MEDITATIONS ON THE PSALMS

BY

REV. RONALD A. KNOX

WITH PREFACE BY

REV. H. S. BOWDEN

OF THE ORATORY

1919

Must Have Books
503 Deerfield Place
Victoria, BC
V9B 6G5
Canada

ISBN: 9781773237596

Copyright 2021 – Must Have Books

TO

L. L.

PREFACE

NOT as a commentary, with its treatment of each successive verse, these meditations consider each Psalm as containing one leading idea, thus forming a unity in itself. Seeing the numerous subjects each Psalm contains, the recognition of this leading idea or formative principle must require deep reflection and close logical reasoning to trace its development to the exclusion of all else.

We are glad to notice in the present volume the same firmness of conviction and robust faith that appear in the author's apologetic works, and that his meditations, with their three points, tend to form solid virtues rather than sentimental affections. He faces squarely objections as they occur. For instance to the permission of evil, of pain and sorrow, the most popular argument against the existence of a good God, he replies that evil is permitted to teach us detachment—that earth is not our home—and to prepare us for eternity.

Bossuet gives two guides for understanding the Psalms. First, God as First Cause. The Psalmist seems to see him not by inference or argument but immediately, within the veil. Thus, in the phenomena of nature, his voice in the thunderstorm breaks the cedars, even the cedars of Lebanon:

in the fathomless ocean deep calls upon deep " in the voice of *thy* cataracts." So in the moral order he alone is blessed who fears God, and the false gods are mocked ; they have eyes and see not, ears and hear not, they are dumb and useless, but the House of Israel hopeth in the Lord. Then, David himself presents the vicissitudes of human life. From an obscure shepherd boy he is appointed King by God, is a mighty victor firm on his throne, then his people in revolt, himself a fugitive from his rebel son, all against him at home and abroad. These dangers without are repeated within : David the saint passes from innocence to sin, from sin to penance, and shews the love of God for a pure soul, his anger when offended, the punishment threatened—again, the sweet consolation that comes with contrition and the cry for pardon. All this is mirrored in the Psalms.

These meditations insist (Ps. 83. *Quam dilecta*) on the value of the interior life as our home, our journey, and our progess, holiness even in a low degree being worth the struggle. It is approached (Ps. 24. *Ad te Domine levavi*) with the sense of our own unworthiness, with confidence in God's mercy, with consciousness of our great needs. Discouragement is to be met by gratitude for our conversion from sin, and for the fact that we are forgiven and in God's grace. We must hope in God though we pass through a valley of spiritual death. Yielding to depression is faithlessness to God. Throughout the meditations a high ideal is put before us. The Church never says " It is enough," but always gives grace for further advance. The detachment proper to Catholics is based on the fact that they are exiles from home and are longing for their release (Ps. 136. *Super flumina*).

The meditations on the Sacraments, the mysteries, and the feasts, complete the book for notes of sermons, and should be of much value to the preacher as well as for private devotions.

H. S. BOWDEN.

NIHIL OBSTAT:

EDWARDUS CAN. MYERS,
Censor deputatus.

IMPRIMATUR:

EDM. CAN. SURMONT
Vic. Gen.

Westmonasterii die 15 Julii 1919.

AUTHOR'S PREFACE

THESE meditations, some of which were originally committed to writing merely for the author's own future reference, are his own reflexions, designed for his own use, on the Sacred Text. He was encouraged by friends to publish them in case they might be of use to those who, while preferring to go back to the Scriptures themselves for their subjects of meditation, find nevertheless that the intellectual preparation demanded for such an exercise does not come easy to them if they undertake it without assistance. The suggestions, therefore, to be found in this book are suggestions merely, and should be regarded as bearing to their original something the same relation as the "hints" given to schoolboys for their Latin Verses bear to the original poem. In a word, they are meant to be used at the overnight preparation rather than in the course of meditation itself.

The text of the Psalms given on the alternate pages is that of the ordinary Douai version ; in some places it does not preserve the exact shade of meaning which the author thought he saw in the Latin text, but it seemed hard to depart from it in view of the fact that it has become familiar to so many Catholics. In closely following the Vulgate, this text represents the Greek of the Septuagint, not the Hebrew which, dating as a written document from a later period, has formed the basis of other translations. In a few cases, where a difference of rendering in the Hebrew has been preserved in the marginal notes to the Douai version, the difference has been taken into account. Apart from these marginal notes no commentary was used for the exposition of the Psalms, but it was naturally impossible not to be influenced by innumerable associations derived from various spiritual authors; and nothing in this book either claims originality or pretends to any superiority if it differs from the interpretations usually given.

The arrangement of the Psalms is designed (roughly) to proceed from the less to the more " interior " levels of the spiritual life. Consequently it hardly needs to be said that in the latter part of the book borrowed lights predominate over personal experience, and more scrupulous care has been taken not to read into the original any sense which, on the ordinary principles of allegorical or mystical interpretation, it could not reasonably be supposed to carry. Except in the case of the last four meditations, Psalms have been chosen which were neither too long nor too short to form one meditation each; they have, for convenience, been distributed in each case into three parts, and a few acts, etc., have been added at the end, but it would not be difficult to use them on a less formal system.

R. A. KNOX.

St. Edmund's College,
Old Hall, Ware.

CONTENTS

I. THE CHRISTIAN LIFE

CONTENTS

III. THE INTERIOR LIFE

IV. SONGS OF ASCENTS

The heavens shew forth the glory of God ; and the firmament declareth the work of his hands.

Day to day uttereth speech ;

and night to night sheweth knowledge.

There are no speeches nor languages, where their voices are not heard ; their sound hath gone forth into all the earth, and their words unto the ends of the world.

He hath set his tabernacle in the sun ; and he, as a bride-groom coming out of his bride chamber,hath rejoiced as a giant to run the way. His going out is from the end of heaven, and his circuit even to the end thereof, and there is no one that can hide himself from his heat.

The law of the Lord is unspotted, converting souls,

the testimony of the Lord is faithful, giving wisdom to little ones.

The justices of the Lord are right, rejoicing

1. Ps. XVIII. (Caeli enarrant).

GOD'S THREEFOLD REVELATION OF HIMSELF TO MAN.

FIRST POINT. *God revealed by his creation.* The whole of creation speaks to us of the Cause that produced it ; but the heavens especially, where we can read the vastness of God's operation (and therefore of his being) as well as the perfect order, which can only be attributed to supreme Wisdom. He reveals himself in the light, that is, in truths that are manifest even to our earthly intelligence ; and equally in the darkness, that is, by the mysteries which baffle us and so make us acknowledge an Intelligence superior to our own. These lights and shadows of creation are God's first missionaries ; no one can plead, even in heathen countries, that the truth of God's existence was not thus proposed to him. And as the temporal symbol of his own power, which at once sustains and vivifies and enlightens the whole universe, he has given us the sun, centre of the whole system in which our world moves, penetrating everywhere with its heat and light, as God himself is everywhere present in substance and in operation.

SECOND POINT. *God revealed in the Christian dispensation.* The details of the Christian dispensation, though many of them are such that we must obey them in blind faith, not by knowledge, yet claim our homage by their perfect order and beauty. His moral law, so unswerving, appealing so readily to all our highest instincts ; the manner of his revelation, adapted to the simple and ignorant as well as to the learned ; the generosity of the rewards he offers ; the special counsels, through

hearts, the commandment of the Lord is light-some, enlightening the eyes.

The fear of the Lord is holy, enduring for ever and ever, the judgments of the Lord are true, justified in themselves, more to be desired than gold and many precious stones, and sweeter than honey and the honeycomb.

For thy servant keepeth them, and in keeping them there is a great reward.

Who can understand sins ?

From my secret ones cleanse me, O Lord,

and from those of others spare thy servant.

If they shall have no dominion over me, then shall I be without spot, and I shall be cleansed from the greatest sin.

And the words of my mouth shall be such as may please, and the meditation of my heart always in thy sight,

O Lord, my helper, and my redeemer.

the observance of which he leads devout souls to great spiritual enlightenment ; the terrible punishments he threatens to the disobedient ; the moral values he teaches us (the importance of motives, the refusal to respect persons, etc.), all plainly self-justified, and yet to us so difficult and so desirable of attainment—in all these he makes himself known to us, and more fully in proportion as we observe them more carefully, since " he that doeth the works shall know the doctrine."

THIRD POINT. *God revealed in the human conscience.* But there is a third revelation, this time clearly progressive according to our souls' state—his revelation in the individual conscience. How hard it is for our fallen nature to appreciate its own degradation, and estimate its own sins aright ! We must ask to be delivered from the pride and sloth which make us unconscious of sin, the acquiescence in worldly standards which deadens us to its significance. Only when our spiritual vision is thus cleared shall we be delivered from that sin which is the most dangerous, because the underlying cause, of all our sins—the pride of the human spirit. How they avail with God, the prayers (whether vocal or mental) of those whose consciences are truly illuminated ! Let us pray that as he has redeemed us from the dominion of sin, so he will ever help us forward towards such inward perfection.

Acts—Faith in God and in his revelation ; gratitude for his having revealed himself ; desire for an enlightened conscience.

Colloquy with God as the Sun of our lives.

Lord, thou hast proved me and known me ;

thou hast known my sitting down and my rising up.

Thou hast understood my thoughts afar off ;

my path and my line thou hast searched out.

And thou hast foreseen all my ways ; for there is no speech in my tongue.

Behold, O Lord, thou hast known all things, the last and those of old ;

thou hast formed me, and hast laid thy hand upon me.
Thy knowledge is become wonderful for me ; it is high, and I cannot reach to it.

Whither shall I go from thy Spirit ? Or whither shall I flee from thy face ? If I ascend up into Heaven, thou art there ; if I descend into hell, thou art there.

If I take to me the wings of the morning, and dwell in the uttermost parts of the sea, even there also shall thy hand lead me, and thy right hand shall hold me.

2. Ps. CXXXVIII. (Domine probasti).

SOME ATTRIBUTES OF GOD.

FIRST POINT. *The omniscience of God.* I am on my trial, under the scrutiny of the all-seeing eye which no motion of mine can escape. My ordinary daily actions, so trivial that I myself am hardly conscious of them, are present to the consciousness of God. More, he understands my thoughts, the inmost thoughts of a creature, infinitely below him in dignity ; he understands my secret motives, though I myself am often blind to the nature of them. Further, he can foresee all that will befal me, my temptations, my sins, my place in eternity. He needs no words of mine to acquaint him with what I am. His eternal wisdom planned the whole scheme of creation, before Time was, and can reach forward into the fathomless depths of eternity, foreknowing the destiny of every individual soul. When he created me, he arranged all the circumstances of my life that were to test my loyalty, or lead me to him. With what utter submission of spirit must I bow to his Will for me !

SECOND POINT. *The omnipresence and omnipotence of God.* God is a spirit, confined by no limitations of space ; everywhere he is present, witnessing all that passes. If by his mercy I attain to heaven, it will be to enjoy his full presence; if I am condemned to eternal punishment, it will be by a personal exercise of his power. By some hasty flight to a distant country the criminal may, perhaps, escape from human ken ; he will never travel far enough to escape from God's hand, that still guides his path, still controls his destinies. The sinner may protect himself from the world's

And I said, Perhaps darkness shall cover me ;
and night shall be my light in my pleasures.
But darkness shall not be dark to thee, and
night shall be light as the day ; the darkness
thereof and the light thereof are alike to thee.

For thou hast possessed my reins ; thou hast
protected me from my mother's womb : I
will praise thee, for thou art fearfully magnified ;
wonderful are thy works, and my soul knoweth
right well. My bone is not hid from thee,
which thou hast made in secret, and my substance in the lower parts of the earth. Thy
eyes did see my imperfect being, and in thy
book shall all be written ; days shall be formed
and no one in them.

But to me thy friends, O God, are made
exceedingly honourable ; their principality is
exceedingly strengthened. I will number them
and they shall be multiplied above the sand.

I rose up, and am still with thee.

If thou wilt kill the wicked, O God, ye men
of blood, depart from me ; because you say in
thought, They shall receive thy cities in vain.

Lord, have I not hated them that hate thee ?
And pined away . because of thy enemies ?
I have hated them with a perfect hatred, and
they are become enemies to me.

Prove me, O God, and know my heart ;
examine me, and know my paths.

And see if there be in me the way of iniquity,
and lead me in the eternal way.

scandal by covering up in darkness the guilty life he leads ; but to God the darkness and the light are alike ; he is close at hand, even where human observation is impossible. Nor is God present merely as a witness ; he is everywhere present in his unlimited Power, which equally calls for our humble adoration. If it is wonderful that we cannot hide ourselves from him now, still more wonderful was the hidden process by which he brought us into being ; he made us from the dust, he knew our fashioning in the womb, our whole lives are as it were chronicled before him ; he reigned in solitary majesty before Time was, or the human race began.

THIRD POINT. *The justice of God.* One of God's attributes will only be fully made known to us in the future—his infallible justice. The time will come when his friends, often so poor and despised on earth, will shine as stars in the firmament, the innumerable company of just men made perfect. His knowledge, his presence, his power will all make themselves felt at the day of the Resurrection. And at the same time his righteous judgment will be exercised against the sinners, who despised their birthright and made light of their celestial citizenship. O, that I might learn to see things with God's eyes ; that I might be blind to all the transitory allurements of the world, and hate sin as he hates it ! May he prove me with his trials until he sees my heart as he would have it be ; may his grace put me continually in mind of my sins, and disclose to me my impure motives ; may he never spare me, as long as he sees in me aught that offends him, till he has set my feet safely on the path of eternal life !

Bless the Lord, O my soul, and let all that is within me bless his holy name.

Bless the Lord, O my soul, and never forget all he hath done for thee; who forgiveth all thy iniquities,

who healeth all thy diseases.

Who redeemeth thy life from destruction,

who crowneth thee with mercy and compassion.

Who satisfieth thy desire with good things;

thy youth shall be renewed like the eagle's.

The Lord doth mercies and judgment for all that suffer wrong.

He hath made his ways known to Moses, his wills to the children of Israel.

Acts : Congratulation with God on his per-fections ; fear of offending his all-seeing eye ; hatred of our sins.

Colloquy with the ever-present Witness who knows all the secrets of our hearts.

3. Ps. CII. (Benedic anima mea, Dominum ; et omnia).

UNIVERSALITY OF THE MERCIES OF GOD.

FIRST POINT. *God's mercy is all-sufficing.* All that is within me, bless God's name—not merely my lips or even my affections, but my will, my intellect, my every action : he claims *all*, who gives *all*, and it is God who has done *all* for me. He forgives *all* my sins—not merely *all* the debt inherited from my first parents, or *all* the sins of my youth, but the sins by which I still offend him every day. He heals *all* my diseases, *all* the way-ward passions, *all* the inordinate affections, *all* the weakness in purpose and in prayer, of those who truly devote themselves to him. To have rescued me from eternal punishment, is not that to do *all* for me ? And yet he does more ; he crowns his gift with the promise of an eternal reward ; and even on earth he adds to these favours spiritual delights, enabling by his grace that free activity of the soul which (like the exercise of man's natural faculties) carries with it is own gratification.

SECOND POINT. *God's mercy is all-embracing.* God does not victimize this or that soul for the general good, does not act by rough and ready measures. He cares for *all*, and even when he allows wrong to triumph, he has a merciful purpose for its victims ; just as he allowed the children of Israel to be persecuted by the Egyptians in order

The Lord is compassionate and merciful, long-suffering and plenteous in mercy; he will not always be angry, nor will he threaten for ever.

He hath not dealt with us according to our sins, nor rewarded us according to our iniquities.

For according to the height of the heaven above the earth, he hath strengthened his mercy towards them that fear him;

As far as the East is from the West, so far hath he removed our iniquities from us.

As a father hath compassion on his children, so hath the Lord compassion on them that fear him,

For he knoweth our frame; he remembereth that we are dust.

Man's days are as grass; as the flower of the field so shall he flourish; for the spirit shall pass in him, and he shall know his place no more.

But the mercy of the Lord is from eternity and unto eternity, upon them that fear him, and his justice unto children's children, to such as keep his covenant, and are mindful of his commandments to do them.

The Lord hath prepared his throne in heaven, and his kingdom shall rule over all. Bless the Lord, all ye his Angels, you that are mighty in strength, and execute his word, hearkening to the voice of his orders; bless the Lord, all ye his hosts, you ministers of his that do his

that they might acquire the racial spirit of independence which was necessary to the people , destined to preserve his oracles. Even when he punishes our sins, the punishments (in this world) are not for *all* time, but only until we repent and amend—and this although our sins, when they represent a deliberate turning away from him, of themselves deserve infinite punishment. Here is one of the mystical meanings of the Cross ; the length of its stem represents .the infinite condescension by which God bridged *all* the gulf between himself and man ; the width of its arms represents the infinite distance between man sinful and man redeemed, *all* the difference between West and East, that is, between darkness and light. His love has none of the selfishness which the passion of human love often shews ; his is the love of a Father, who has mercy on *all* his children, not one more than another ; and, because he knows the special weaknesses and special temptations of *all*, makes allowances for *all* according to the frailty of their composition.

THIRD POINT. *God's mercy is for all time.* What is man ? With his limited powers, his limited knowledge, his faculties which decline, might we not have thought that his being is limited to the brief time he enjoys on earth ? But it is not so ; in return for our imperfect adoration, our uncertain fidelity, our fitful recollectedness and firmness of purpose, God promises the continuance of his mercies for *all* eternity. For the God who thus engages our gratitude is *all*-powerful ; in blessing him for his goodness, we unite ourselves with *all* the angels who carry out his decrees by the delegation of his own power, with *all* the blessed

B

will; bless the Lord, all his works, in every place of his dominion.

O my soul, bless thou the Lord.

O Lord our Lord, how admirable is thy name in the whole earth!

For thy magnificence is elevated above the heavens.

Out of the mouth of infants and of sucklings thou hast perfected praise, because of thy

spirits that stand round his throne and serve him, with *all* the dumb creatures that, fulfilling his will in their several functions, contribute to the great chorus of his praise. And I, raised above the lesser creatures by the possession of an immortal soul, more bound in gratitude than the Angels, because not only created but redeemed by him— shall not I begin on earth the adoration which I am to pay in eternity ?

Acts : Thanksgiving for God's several mercies, especially for our Redemption ; adoration of God's Omnipotence.

Colloquy with God as my Father, who, though caring alike for all, cares for me individually.

4. Ps. VIII. (Domine Dominus noster).
THE DIGNITY OF MAN.

FIRST POINT. *God shews his omnipotence by the weakness of the earthly instruments he uses.* Whether we consider the mere fact of existence, and argue from the greatness of the universe even as we know it to the greatness of its Creator ; or whether from its infinite variety we admire the wonderful delicacy of his work in the petal or the snowflake ; or whether from its harmony and order we infer the wisdom of the eternal Mind that disposed it, we are forced to our knees in admiration of God's power. Not that this exhausts his greatness, for the effect must be less than, not equal to, the Cause ; from the magnificence of creation we infer a Magnificence still greater beyond it. And that Magnificence is equally displayed in the history of God's dealing with men ; lest it should be thought that he depends in any way upon the

enemies, that thou mayest destroy the enemy
and the avenger.

For I will behold thy heavens, the works of
thy fingers : the moon and the stars which thou
hast founded.

What is man that thou art mindful of him ?

Or the son of man, that thou visitest him ?

Thou hast made him a little less than the
angels.

Thou hast crowned him with glory and honour,
and hast set him over the works of thy hands ;
thou hast subjected all things under his feet,
all sheep and oxen, moreover the beasts also of
the fields, the birds of the air, and the fishes of
the sea that pass through the paths of the sea.

strength or the wisdom of his human agents, he has chosen the weak things of the world, modest women, souls hidden away in the cloister, men of little education and inferior natural gifts, to shew forth his sanctity and to win souls for him—St. Theresa, St. Bruno, the Curé d'Ars, etc.

SECOND POINT. *Man, even considered in himself, is insignificant compared with the universe around him.* The vast realms of space, the heavenly bodies that comprise not merely other worlds but other systems, yet are all fashioned delicately as if by a craftsman's fingers, seem to dwarf man and throw him into the shade. Can it be that a single species (among the many living species) of a single planet (among many planets) of a solar system (among many solar systems) is the object of special care, watchfulness, and jealousy on the part of God ? Nay, that God himself, taking the form of a member of that species, lived on earth and toiled and suffered to redeem it ; that his Holy Spirit loves to dwell specially in the hearts of the sons of men ? So it is ; for God, not content with the myriad spirits that surround him, praise him, and do his will, formed yet other spirits, mysteriously bound up with material bodies, to serve him on earth.

THIRD POINT. *Man is the priest of nature.* Owing to the special faculties with which God has endowed him, Man, though fallen, has become the master of the brute creation, and tamed to his own purposes the brutes that excel him in strength ; nay, he can tunnel under the earth, ride through the air, chain waterfalls, navigate the depths of the sea. But above all, Man, unlike the rest of creation, is intellectual and the object of his own thought. And because he is thus endowed with

O Lord our Lord, how admirable is thy name in all the earth !

Blessed is the man who hath not walked in the counsel of the ungodly,

nor stood in the way of sinners,

nor sat in the chair of pestilence.

But his will is in the law of the Lord,

and on his law he shall meditate day and night.

intellect and purposive will, it is the privilege and duty of man to offer consciously to God the praises which the whole chorus of creation mutely proclaims on every side. In all the earth God's name is admirable ; over all the earth, wherever the human race dwells, God would have Man for his priest. What dignity has God conferred on us, my soul, that we should take our share in this continual oblation !

Acts : Admiration of God's power and wisdom : gratitude for our creation and for our creation as sentient beings.

Colloquy with God our Creator, who made the universe out of nothing.

5. Ps. I. (Beatus vir).

A CAUTION AGAINST WORLDLINESS.

FIRST POINT. *The soul must, in its measure, retire into seclusion from the world.* Blessed is the man who has not *walked* in the counsel, that is, according to the lights and standards, of the imperfect world around him ; who has not voluntarily gone out of his way into sinful courses. But we must not be content with this, we must walk in the right way, not *standing* about irresolutely and parleying with sin, by encouraging occasions, evil imaginations, etc. Nor must we even *sit down*, that is, sink into apathy about spiritual things and fall back into acquiescence with the promptings of our own nature ; for ours is a fallen nature, and we have to flee from its indifference towards heaven as if from a spot contaminated by disease. The will must be trained by mortification to run counter to our natural inclinations and conform itself to the higher law of grace ; the mind must be schooled by meditation on the mysteries of the faith, alike

And he shall be like a tree,

which is planted near the running waters,

·which shall bring forth its fruit in due season.
And his leaf shall not fall off ;

and all whatsoever he shall do shall prosper.

Not so the wicked, not so, but like the dust which the wind driveth from the face of the earth.

Therefore the wicked shall not rise again in judgment, nor sinners in the council of the just.

For the Lord knoweth the way of the just, and the way of the wicked shall perish.

in times of happiness and in times of distress, lest we should forget our high calling.

SECOND POINT. *Only the mortified life is fruitful.* In nature itself, it is not the least tended trees that are the healthiest, the pollarded willow thrives from the very harshness of its treatment. And the mortified life is to be compared to such a tree, rooted in one spot and yet continually growing : it does not depend on accidents of rain and drought, of happiness, that is, or of misfortune, because it is planted by the waters of God's grace, flowing like a river, always the same yet always mysteriously fresh. Fed by such nourishment, it will bring forth the fruit of holiness in due season, when God sees fit and in the measure he ordains. This fruit of holiness is the only produce of it which matters in the light of eternity : but even the leaves, that is the outward and unessential part of our lives, our temporal happiness, will be blessed by God's special favour ; and the works we undertake in his honour will be prospered through his Providence, often beyond our knowing.

THIRD POINT. *The immortified life is sterile and transient.* The mortified life is the seed which falls into the ground and, buried as it is, grows into a flourishing plant. The life of the worldly, for all its appearance of freedom, is like the chaff or dust which the wind scatters about, unstable in principle and barren of fruit. It is the stubble which, as St. Paul tells us, will be burned in the fire of judgment. Already, St. John warns us, God's fan is in his hand, and he will one day burn the chaff with unquenchable fire. Happy are we if we walk in the way of the just, over which, however perilous it may seem, the Providence of God

Lord, who shall dwell in thy tabernacle ?

Or who shall rest in thy holy hill ?

He that walketh without blemish,
and worketh justice.

He that speaketh truth in his heart ;

keeps a fatherly watch for our protection ; if we turn our backs resolutely on the way of sinners, which leads over uncharted ground to the wilderness, the precipice, or the morass.

Acts : Determination to avoid the occasions of sin ; resolve to persevere in the exercises of religion.

Colloquy with God who will judge us by our fruits.

6. Ps. XIV. (Domine, quis habitabit).
JUSTICE TOWARDS OUR NEIGHBOUR.

FIRST POINT. *No one can truly approach perfection till his common faults are conquered.* The tabernacle of God among his ancient people was approached by a court, where stood the brazen altar on which sacrifices were made for sin—as if to symbolize the purity demanded of the ministers before they should enter the holy place. So it is with all who would strive after sanctification ; they have to strive first of all to purge themselves of the sins that mar their daily life ; the burden that weighs us down, the fetters that clog our feet, must be left behind before we ascend the mountain of perfection, with its finer airs and wider prospects. This does not merely mean caring for our own souls, by avoiding as far as possible the stains left upon our character by the world and the flesh ; we all, to some extent, have our social duties, whose punctual performance must be part of our way of purgation : even if we retired into the cloister, we could not altogether neglect the claims of human society.

SECOND POINT. *The duty of truthfulness.* The heathen philosopher said that the lie on his lips was of little importance ; he only was truly wretched who had the lie in his soul. It is of this

who hath not used deceit in his tongue,

nor done evil to his neighbour,

nor taken up a reproach against his neighbours.

In his sight the malignant is brought to nothing, but he glorifieth them that fear the Lord.

He that sweareth to his neighbours, and deceiveth not ;

he that hath not put out his money to usury,

nor taken bribes against the innocent.

that our Lord speaks when he tells us to have " a single eye " ; no frivolous caprice, no merely personal prejudice, must blind our judgments of men and matters ; we must be honest with ourselves, whether in civic or in private life. And we must speak the truth—not merely by avoiding false statements, but by being careful not to give wrong impressions, not to repeat as a fact what we only know on doubtful authority, and so on. We must do no evil to our neighbour : our Lord has taught us that all the world is our neighbour, but we have especially to watch our conduct towards our rivals and competitors, who are here called our neighbours : do we scrupulously avoid the chances we get of taking an unfair advantage of them ? Do we, when others criticise them and tell stories to their discredit, forget the scandal ; or do we treasure it up and eagerly retail it, regardless whether the interests of truth and charity are served thereby ?

THIRD POINT. *The duty of honesty.* The world around us is full of people who are making money and securing advancement by unscrupulous and even fraudulent means ; the Christian will not even be moved to jealousy of spiritual good ; far less will he imitate these methods. He will regard his promise, once given, as binding, even though it be to his own disadvantage. He will use his worldly wealth as a stewardship from God, contributing to the needs of the poor and of the Church, avoiding " gambling " investments, careful, as far as he may be, that he is not, either as employer or as customer, deriving profit from the ill-paid or over-driven labour of others. He will not let his free judgment, either in public or in

He that doeth these things shall not be moved
for ever.

Blessed are they whose iniquities are forgiven

and whose sins are covered.

Blessed is the man to whom the Lord hath
not imputed sin,
and in whose spirit there is no guile.

Because I was silent

my bones grew old,
whilst I cried out all the day long.

For day and night thy hand was heavy upon
me; I am turned in my anguish, whilst the
thorn is fastened. [*In the Hebrew this reads*
" My moisture is turned into the droughts of
the summer."]

private life, be biassed through fear, favour, or worldly advantage. These habits of truth and honesty, so often neglected, ought to be the sure foundation of the Christian's conduct.

Acts : Detestation of falsehood and dishonesty ; resolve to examine carefully the claims of justice on our conscience ; prayer for innocence.

Colloquy with God who is the Truth, and has no respect of persons.

7. Ps. XXXI. (Beati quorum).
THE BLESSINGS OF A GOOD CONSCIENCE.

FIRST POINT. *The misery of unconfessed sin on the conscience.* Blessed are those who have their sins *first* forgiven by God, and *then* " covered up," put away from sight. The law of the Christian conscience is that sin must be first revealed to God, if he is to consent to hide it, *i.e.* to count it against us no longer : if we attempt to hide it without forgiveness, we find that we have become false at the roots of our being ; all our behaviour is an acted lie. While we hold our tongues—cherish the memory of our sin, yet try to put a good face on it and live as if we were no different from our neighbours,—the whole fabric of our spiritual life seems to rot away, and, in spite of our outward silence, there is something in us that *cries out* unceasingly. The hand of God, stretched out in chastisement, becomes burdensome to us. We feel a spiritual pain that, like a thorn in the flesh, will not let us forget its presence (or, according to the Hebrew, our moisture is turned into drought ; *i.e.* all our prayers and exercises become intolerable to us from aridity).

I have acknowledged my sin to thee, and my injustice I have not concealed.

I said, I will confess against myself injustice to the Lord,

and thou hast forgiven the iniquity of my sin.

For this shall everyone that is holy pray to thee in a seasonable time,

And yet in a flood of many waters they shall not come nigh unto him.

Thou art my refuge from the trouble which hath encompassed me; my joy, deliver me from them that surround me.

I will give thee understanding,
and I will instruct thee in this way in which thou shalt go;

I will fix mine eyes upon thee.

Do not become like the horse and the mule who have no understanding.

With bit and bridle bind fast their jaws, who come not nigh unto thee.

SECOND POINT. *The wisdom of setting the troubled conscience at rest voluntarily, without wait- for God's warnings.* It is the part of wisdom, to acknowledge our fault instead of trying to eal it from ourselves and from God. It should be a spontaneous voice within us—the voice of a well-directed conscience—not any pressure from outside, that leads us to this resolution ; if perfect interior contrition has been elicited, with the resolution to submit our sins to the tribunal, God forgives our sins *at once.* For this gift of contrition the Christian soul should pray " in a seasonable time ", *i.e.* as soon as possible after the commission of the sin, and *before* we begin to be warned by calamities, public or private, by the fear of death, etc. For although God's chastise- ments are meant for our correction, it is not easy for the soul which has not disciplined itself in calmer times to rise suddenly to a consciousness of God's claims upon us : the outward pressure of grief, fear, anxiety etc. may easily, in the case of the undisciplined soul, have a merely numbing effect. It is the soul already at peace with God that can find in him a refuge in tribulation and a source of holy joy when there is misery all round.

THIRD POINT. *The perfect conscience serves God freely without need of coercion.* God promises the faithful soul, which tries to serve him, *understand- ing, i.e.* enlightenment of the conscience which naturally prefers what is pleasing to him, and *instruction, i.e.* guidance in the course that is best for it ; a mere glance of his eye, as it were, will be enough to restrain or to encourage it. We are not to be like the dumb beasts, which serve mechani- cally and need constant correction—such are the

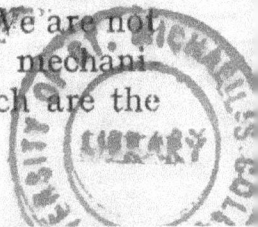

Many are the scourges of the sinner, but mercy shall encompass him that hopeth in the Lord.

Be glad in the Lord and rejoice, ye just, and glory, all ye right of heart.

Have mercy on me, O God, according to thy great mercy, and according to the multitude of thy tender mercies, blot out my iniquity.

Wash me yet more from my iniquity, and cleanse me from my sin.

For I know my iniquity, and my sin is always before me.

To thee only have I sinned, and have done evil before thee,

that thou mayst be justified in thy words, and mayst overcome when thou art judged.

worldly, whose will God overrules instead of ruling it, and the imperfect souls which have constantly to be checked by the Divine chastisements. To those who serve God freely, the troubles which exasperate the worldly and distress the sinner become mortifications, which do not for a moment lessen their sense of his all-embracing mercies. Let us then strive to attain that *rightness of the heart*, which alone can interpret God's ways and enable us to be joyful even in our time of pilgrimage.

Acts : Contrition for past sins, desire for true illumination of the conscience.

Colloquy with God who invites us to be his friends, though he can exact unwilling service.

8. Ps. L. (Miserere).

CONTRITION FOR SIN.

FIRST POINT. *Motives for asking forgiveness.* On God's side, there is no motive I can appeal to in demanding pardon except his own infinite mercy : what but infinite mercy could be commensurate with the injury my sin has done him ? Once more, after so many repentances and so many resolutions, I must appeal to the same source of grace. What can I do but acknowledge my misery ? Would that the consciousness of it might never leave me. It is not that I have failed, that I have disappointed myself, that I am ashamed of men's judgment, even of the priest's in the confessional : it is the insult to the Divine Majesty, the soiling of the Divine image in me, the thwarting of the Divine Will for me, that constitutes my sin. Thou, God, hast seen me, and I have forgotten thy presence : thou hast warned me, and I have

For behold, I was conceived in iniquities, and in my sins did my mother conceive me.

For behold, thou hast loved truth; the uncertain and hidden things of thy wisdom thou hast made manifest to me.

Thou shalt sprinkle me with hyssop, and I shall be cleansed; thou shalt wash me, and I shall be made whiter than snow.

To my hearing thou shalt give joy and gladness, and the bones that have been humbled shall rejoice.

Turn thy face away from my sins,

and blot out all my iniquities.

Create a clean heart in me, O God, and renew a right spirit within my bowels.

Cast me not away from thy face, and take not thy holy spirit from me.

Restore to me the joy of thy salvation, and strengthen me with a perfect spirit.

I will teach the unjust thy ways, and the wicked shall be converted to thee.

Deliver me from blood, O God, thou God of my salvation, and my tongue shall extol thy justice.

neglected and justified thy warnings. True, I have inherited from my first parents a fallen nature ; but thou, in thy faithfulness, didst reveal thyself anew to me and strengthen me, through my Saviour's Passion, with the hidden treasures of thy grace, and yet—I have sinned.

SECOND POINT. *Prayer for remission of sin.* As the High Priest sprinkled the people with the blood of victims, so the Blood of my Saviour is an eternal fountain of pardon ; wash me in this Blood, that my discoloured soul may be clean once more. Oh how gracious are the words of pardon which thou, through the priest, wilt bestow on me ! According to the measure in which I now humble myself with true contrition, thou wilt gladden my heart with fresh grace. My sins, though there be yet a penalty to pay for them, will no longer be the object of thy indignant regard ; the sentence decreed against me will be annulled as with a stroke of the pen ; more than this, thou wilt convey to me in the sacrament of Penance active grace, to resist my sins in the future and live more worthily of thee. O may I never merit the dreadful judgment of being cast away for ever from before thee ! Inspire me always with thy Holy Spirit, that I may avoid such condemnation ; renew and strengthen in me the grace bestowed on me in baptism by my Saviour's Death.

THIRD POINT. *Resolve for the future and prayer for grace.* From henceforth I desire nothing better than to live worthily of these benefits, and set an example of justice towards my neighbour and piety towards thee. Without thy pardon, indeed, I could do nothing ; I should be like the blood-guilty outlaw who has no City of Refuge to flee to.

O Lord, thou wilt open my lips, and my mouth shall declare thy praise.

For if thou hadst desired sacrifice, I would indeed have given it; with burnt offerings thou wilt not be delighted.

A sacrifice to God is an afflicted spirit; a contrite and humbled heart, O God, thou wilt not despise.

Deal favourably, O Lord, in thy good will with Sion, that the walls of Jerusalem may be built up.

Then shalt thou accept the sacrifice of justice, oblations and whole burnt offerings; then shall they lay calves upon thy altar.

Lord, thou hast blessed thy land; thou hast turned away the captivity of Jacob.

Thou hast forgiven the iniquity of thy people; thou hast covered all their sins.

Thou hast mitigated all thy anger; thou hast turned away from the wrath of thy indignation.

Convert us, O God our Saviour, and turn off thy anger from us.

Wilt thou be angry with us for ever? Or wilt thou extend thy wrath from generation to generation?

But with the help of thy grace to move and inspire me, I will begin to live to thy glory ; not by a multitude of offerings, not by performing heroic sacrifices (though it would be my bounden duty, didst thou require it), but by the submission of a humbled will, by a heart that has learned, through experience of contrition, to distrust its own strength. The defences of my soul are, indeed, sadly laid waste, but thy power can raise them anew, stronger than before ; and under this protection, restored to a state of grace, I will endeavour to do thee the service that is thy due, offering all my best thoughts and actions with the sole intention of thy glory.

Acts : Acknowledgment of sin, full contrition, resolution to live for God's glory.

Colloquy with the Lamb of God, who has washed us in his Blood.

9.   Ps. LXXXIV. (Benedixisti, Domine).
CONSIDERATIONS ON ABSOLUTION.

FIRST POINT. *Thanksgiving for relief.* I am released from sin, as the earth is released from the chill of winter, or prisoners from the bitterness of captivity. My account is discharged ; my past, by the favour of God, lies buried and counts against me no more in eternity. All this is but the expression of the fact that God, eternally just, has ceased to look down on my soul in indignation ; I have made my peace with him, and that is all that matters in life or death. Oh may this return to him be a real return, so that I shall never again deserve his anger ! But for this gift of absolution, I had merited (and may yet merit by renewed sin) not a passing frown, but a reprobation which is as

Thou wilt turn, O God, and bring us to life,
and thy people shall rejoice in thee.

Shew us, O Lord, thy mercy, and grant us
thy salvation.
I will hear what the Lord God will speak in
me,
for he will speak peace unto his people,

and unto his saints, and unto them that are
converted to the heart.

Surely his salvation is near to them that fear
him, that glory may dwell in our land.

Mercy and truth have met each other ; justice
and peace have kissed.

eternal and changeless as the eternity and change-lessness of God. See, my soul, how near we have been to the brink of eternal ruin ; learn at once thy peril and his infinite goodness.

SECOND POINT. *Petition for renewed grace.* But the remission of God's anger is not all that he does for us in absolution. Well for us that it is not ; for, by our sins, we have stopped the channels of his grace ; and it would avail us little to be discharged of guilt, if those channels were to remain shut from us still. Recovery is not merely the cessation of sickness, but the building anew of wasted tissues, the return of the body's powers to the enjoyment of their normal functions. This, too, absolution gives us ; and it is in the conscious-ness of these renewed powers that we find proof of our restoration. Lord, let me learn from this experience to listen at all times to the voice of conscience by which thou speakest to me ; let me never forget that peace with thee depends upon living and active membership of thy chosen people, the Church. Let my conversion be no temporary turning aside from sinful ways, but a true conver-sion of the heart, a revolution in my life, an epoch in my history ; that my justification may be, as thou desirest it to be, the beginning of my sanctification.

THIRD POINT. *Confidence in God's mercies.* A few whispered words, a few minutes of penance, and the soul doomed to hell has passed into a soul bound for heaven ! How intimate, then, how condescending, how easily available is the operation of redeeming grace ! The Cross reaches from earth to heaven ; in it the faithfulness of God to his own Nature is mysteriously reconciled with

Truth is sprung out of the earth, and justice hath looked down from heaven.

For the Lord will give goodness, and our earth shall yield her fruit.

Justice shall walk before him, and shall set his steps in the way.

Bring to the Lord, O ye children of God, bring to the Lord the offspring of rams. Bring to the Lord glory and honour, bring to the Lord glory to his name, adore ye the Lord in his holy court.

The voice of the Lord is upon the waters; the God of majesty hath thundered; the Lord upon many waters.

mercy to the sinner, eternal Justice with the reconciliation of our estranged souls to their Creator : God himself is " lifted up from the earth," that God himself may look down from heaven to pardon. Will not the loving-kindness that inspired such a remedy for our sins carry us still further, till the showers of grace produce at last from our barren souls the fruits of good living we have so often promised, so often failed to bring forth ? Will not his justice at last be reproduced in our souls, clearing aside the thick growth of corrupt nature, levelling pride, lifting up our weakness, making ready in the wilderness of our souls a highway for the King to walk on ?

Acts : Fear of sin, resolution of amendment, confidence in God's purpose for our sanctification.

Colloquy with the Good Physician who both heals and restores us.

10. Ps. XXVIII. (Afferte Domino).
THE GIFTS OF THE HOLY SPIRIT.

FIRST POINT. *The gift of the fear of God.* This Psalm describes the effects on nature of a high wind, and finds in them an allegory of the power of God's Holy Spirit. The wind itself, rushing about our ears, seems to invite us to follow its guidance ; so the Holy Spirit invites us to come into God's courts and ask his assistance, bringing with us our best offerings, the most vigorous and the most valued of our natural faculties, to be sanctified by his guidance. The sweep of the wind over the sea reminds us of the time when earth was formless and void, and the Spirit moved upon the face of the waters : the Holy Spirit is God, who created

The voice of the Lord is in power, the voice of the Lord is in magnificence.

The voice of the Lord breaketh the cedars; yea, the Lord shall break the cedars of Libanus, and shall reduce them to pieces as a calf of Libanus, and as the beloved son of unicorns.

The voice of the Lord divideth the flame of fire.

The voice of the Lord shaketh the desert; and the Lord shall shake the desert of Cades.

The voice of the Lord prepareth the stags, and he will discover the thick woods;

all things out of nothing. And as the roaring of the gale and the mountainous waves daunt our courage, they remind us that we should feel a holy *fear* for the God who is infinitely exalted in power above all his creatures, even the most violent of natural forces. Let us fear God's majesty, his almighty power, his unerring judgments.

SECOND POINT. *The gifts of wisdom, knowledge, and understanding.* And now the wind hurries over the forest ; see how the trees all bend in a single direction, and the boughs that cannot bend snap off and are whirled along. So the Holy Spirit would sway the hearts of men in the direction of their sanctification by the gift of true *wisdom*, and would break down the stubborn resistances of foolish nature. A forest fire breaks out, and as we see the flames of it swept this way and that, we are reminded of the divided tongues of fire which appeared at Pentecost, accompanying the wonderful gift of *knowledge* then given to the Apostles, and granted to us in our measure according to our prayers. And now the forest land stops short, and the wind sweeps over the trackless wastes of the wilderness ; not a grain of sand in all the desert but feels this impulse ! Think, then, how the Holy Spirit searches out all things, and how we should pray for the gift of *understanding*, that whatever is dark and difficult to our weak minds may be more fully manifested to us by the omniscient Enlightener of our hearts.

THIRD POINT. *The gifts of counsel, piety, and fortitude.* The wind makes itself felt even in the dense thickets where the deer have taken refuge. So the Holy Spirit discerns everything, and penetrates even to our most secret motives ; let

and in his temple all shall speak his glory.

The Lord maketh the flood to dwell, and the Lord shall sit King for ever. The Lord will give strength to his people,

the Lord will bless his people with peace.

When Israel went out of Egypt, the house of Jacob from a barbarous people,

Judea was made his sanctuary, Israel his dominion.

The sea saw, and fled,

Jordan was turned back.

us pray then for the gift of *counsel*, that our hidden intentions may be directed aright. The wind blows in under the church doors, and drives the incense-smoke to and fro ; let us pray that, through his gift of *piety*, the Holy Spirit will take control of our hearts and inspire our prayers, so that they may be acceptable to God. And so the wind passes out to sea again, and reminds us of the winds by which God abated the Flood, and divided the waters of the Red Sea ; and, conscious of that fatherly protection, we ask for the gift of *fortitude* to keep our hearts high amid the waves of sin and of calamity that surround our mortal life. The face of nature is calm again, and we thank God for the peace he has shed abroad in our hearts and the rest he has promised us hereafter.

Acts: Fear, resignation of our wills; invocation of the Holy Spirit.

Colloquy with the Spirit who discerns every thought of our hearts.

11. Ps. CXIII. (In exitu Israel).
GRACE.

FIRST POINT. *Our Redemption the source of all grace.* The escape of Israel from Egypt, with the ceremonies of the Pasch, is the natural type of our redemption by the sacrifice of Calvary, which brings us out of the alien domination of sin into our true country. And in the act of thus delivering us, Christ has claimed for himself our human nature as his temple and as the battle-ground of his Power. The waves of sin that kept us back from God, a prey to our spiritual enemy, have now closed behind us, and though it still remains for

The mountains skipped like rams, and the hills like the lambs of the flock.

What ailed thee, O thou sea, that thou didst flee, and thou, O Jordan, that thou wast turned back ? Ye mountains, that ye skipped like rams, and ye hills like lambs of the flock ?

At the presence of the Lord the earth was moved, at the presence of the God of Jacob,

who turned the rock' into pools of water, and the stony hill into fountains of waters.

Not to us, O Lord, not to us, but to thy name give glory, for thy mercy and for thy truth's sake,

lest the Gentiles should say, Where is their God ?

But our God is in heaven ; he hath done all things, whatsoever he would. The idols of the Gentiles are silver and gold, the works of the hands of men. They have mouths, and speak not ; they have eyes, and see not ; they have ears, and hear not ; they have noses, and smell not ; they have hands, and feel not ; they have feet, and walk not, neither shall they cry out through their throat.

us to pass the river of death, this too has its
passage sweetened and made easy for us by the
Resurrection. Meanwhile, the mountainous obstacles which stood between our unaided nature
and the performance of any act pleasing to God are
removed from their place, and need not daunt
us any more. By what power is it that these
three great barriers—the guilt of sin, the fear of
death, the frailty of human nature, have all at
once made way for us ?   By the presence in human
flesh and suffering under human conditions of the
same God whom we had offended. And now the
face of the world is changed for us, and life, barren
and dreary though it may still seem, becomes
joyful to us through the streams of sanctifying grace
which flow abundantly from the side of the Crucified.

SECOND POINT. *The Christian religion, alone
among religions, insists on the action of grace at every
turn.* What have we, then, that we have not
received ?   What heroic act can we perform, and
not turn afterwards to thank God for the grace
that enabled us ?   If we insist on human effort,
we only justify the attitude of the unbeliever, who
attributes all the triumphs of Christianity to
unusual application of the natural virtues. The
philosophy of the moderns will deny the existence
of a God transcendent and omnipotent, and seeks
to content us with the doctrine of a vague Pan-
theistic deity, a World-soul, immanent in nature
but not above nature, a God tied by his own laws
and powerless to hear prayers or to exert his power
to save. And those who believe in such half-
religions share the fate of their divinity : the
doctrine of God's grace and God's omnipotence
lost, they find themselves unable to help the world

D

Let them that make them become like unto them, and all such as trust in them.

The house of Israel hath hoped in the Lord ; he is their helper and their protector ;
the house of Aaron hath hoped in the Lord ; he is their helper and their protector ;
they that fear the Lord have hoped in the Lord ; he is their helper and their protector.

The Lord hath been mindful of us, and hath blessed us ;

he hath blessed the house of Israel ;
he hath blessed the house of Aaron ;
he hath blessed all that fear the Lord, both little and great.

May the Lord add blessings upon you, upon you and upon your children.

Blessed be you of the Lord, who made heaven and earth ; the heaven of heaven is the Lord's, but the earth he has given to the children of men.

The dead shall not praise thee, O Lord, nor any of them that go down to hell,

But we that live bless the Lord, from this time now and for ever.

by curbing human passions or stimulating human effort. But the Church still knows where her strength lies, and the simplest of her children understand that they must pray for grace ; the religious, the ascetics, the mystics, for all their heroic endeavours, still attribute everything to God ; and those outside the Church who have not lost this sense of dependence have the best chances of conversion and salvation.

THIRD POINT. *We must co-operate jealously with the grace given to us.* Can we then ever cease to be mindful of God's claims, when he is so continually mindful of us ? We shall have to give a strict account of our graces—whether the habitual grace so lavishly granted to all the Church's children, or the supernatural favours bestowed on God's specially privileged friends, or the motions of actual grace which are given also to those without the Church, nay, even to the abandoned sinner and the deliberate heretic for their conversion. We must spare no effort and no prayer to complete the work of grace in ourselves, and to propagate it among the generation that comes after us. God is absolute Lord of heaven and earth, and he has given us the earth as a garden we must cultivate for him : our time here is our probation, and the grace of repentance is not given to us after death, when by our neglect of grace here we have merited eternal reprobation. Let us then so husband our grace here, that we may give thanks among the redeemed for ever.

Acts : Gratitude, confession of our helplessness, resolve not to fall short of grace.

Colloquy with Christ pierced for us, our Rock in the wilderness.

The Lord ruleth me, and I shall want nothing.

He hath set me in a place of pasture.

He hath brought me up on the water of refreshment :

he hath converted my soul.

He hath led me on the paths of justice, for his own name's sake.

For though I shall walk in the midst of the shadow of death,

12. Ps. XXII. (Dominus regit me).

THE MERCY OF THE SACRAMENTS IN LIFE AND DEATH.

FIRST POINT. *The Sacraments are means of justifying us.* We are the sheep of God's pasture ; his flock ; is it likely, then, that the Good Shepherd should allow us to lack anything that is necessary for attaining the end of our existence ? Silly and defenceless like sheep, our souls need continually to be shepherded along, often in ways they cannot understand. But there is one clear way for all, in which no one can mistake the beneficence of his Providence—the way of the Sacraments : no soul can live without pasture. First, then, he brings us to the waters of Baptism : in these refreshing waters he washes away, at the very opening of our lives, the sin of Adam's descent, and (as a shepherd marks his sheep that he may know them) signs us with his mark, the Cross, printed in his own Precious Blood. But—so frail are we—the bearing of his mark is not enough to keep us safely in his flock, we wander away into sin, and he pursues us and brings us back to himself by conversion, restoring us to a state of grace by the Sacrament of *Penance.* He leads us thus continually into the path of justification, and why ? For his name's sake; he chose us, called us, washed us, renews us, that we may live to his glory.

SECOND POINT. *God's Sacraments are the means of sanctifying us.* The world through which he guides our steps is no place for careless happiness. It is a valley where the shadow of death hangs over us all—that is, not merely death itself,

I will fear no evils, for thou art with me.

Thy rod and thy staff, they have comforted me.

Thou hast prepared a table before me against them that afflict me.

Thou hast anointed my head with oil ;

And my chalice which inebriateth me, how goodly is it !

And thy mercy will follow me all the days of my life :

And that I may dwell in the house of the Lord unto length of days.

but all the ills and tribulations of mortality which death casts before it like a shadow. Yet we are not to be afraid of such afflictions, as if, when the sun is not shining on our lives, his Providence ceased to follow and direct us. The rod that corrects us is also the staff that supports us ; the Sacrament of Penance avails not only to wash away sin, but also to win us grace ; and all our troubles, if we will but accept them as a penance, are effectual means to our sanctification. And lest they should overcome our feeble strength, God is continually renewing us interiorly by our daily food—the Sacrament of *Holy Eucharist*; as the germs of disease have more difficulty in attacking a body that is well fed and nourished, so the temptations our trials bring with them are thrown off more easily when we are daily fortified by Communion.

THIRD POINT. *God's Sacraments the foretaste of our glory.* And when at last the shadow darkens, and death itself is close to us, the mercy of the Sacraments does not cease. When our mortal strength is at its weakest, the Sacrament of *Unction* at once pours balm on our spiritual wounds, and anoints us, as it were, to the Kingly heritage of heaven. And when Christ's Body and Blood are given to us in the Holy Viaticum, we know that we can go " in the strength of that food " until the time when, by his grace, we shall sit down and eat and drink with him in the Kingdom of God. Thus all the days of our life, because we have so little strength in ourselves, we are maintained by his supernatural succour, till in His own House Sacraments are done away, and we are safely folded for all eternity.

Praise the Lord, O Jerusalem; praise thy God, O Sion.

Because he hath strengthened the bolts of thy gates;

he hath blessed thy children within thee.

Who hath placed peace in thy borders,

and filleth thee with the fat of corn.

Who sendeth forth his speech to the earth; his word runneth swiftly. Who giveth snow like wool, scattereth mists like ashes; he

Acts : Gratitude ; desire for Sacramental grace ; preparation for our death-bed.

Colloquy with Christ the Good Shepherd.

13. Ps. CXLVII. (Lauda Jerusalem).

THE BLESSED SACRAMENT.

FIRST POINT. *The Sacrament of Peace.* The Church, in her manifold unity and in the interdependence of all her members, is compared to a city—Jerusalem, the city of Peace. By God's ordinance, the bars of her gates are made fast : her Sacraments are ordained for her own children, and loyalty to her is the prerequisite for participation in them ; the Communion of the Church, precisely because it is marked off by signs and tests, is a real spiritual bond between the faithful. Within that Communion, God has promised us special blessings, but these are, first and foremost, social blessings ; for the receiving of them we need, and by the receiving of them we increase, that grace of charity which is the bond of peace between Christian people. And as the basis of civic harmony is the participation of all in the means of life, so the basis of our Christian harmony is the Bread that is given us from heaven, the Body and Blood of Christ received in the Eucharist : the Church is his mystical Body, and it is by the sacramental partaking of his human Body that she becomes ever more closely incorporated with him.

SECOND POINT. *The Sacrament of Life.* For our sakes, the Word of God was made Flesh ; and as, at the first touch of spring, the winter snows begin to thaw and the frost to relax its

sendeth his ice like morsels : who shall stand
before the face of his cold ?

He shall send out his word, and shall melt
them ;

his wind shall blow,
and the waters shall run.

Who declareth his word to Jacob, his justices
and his judgments to Israel.

He hath not done in like manner to every
nation, and his judgments he hath not made
manifest to them.

grip, so in the Incarnation of Jesus Christ the chains of sin that bound us fell away, and the paralysis of our human nature, powerless for good, gave place to fulness of life and spiritual energy. Yet, through our own refusals of grace, we have again and again withdrawn ourselves from the genial warmth of grace, grown hard and inert under the chilling influence of sin. Thanks be to God for the word of absolution that has freed and softened our hearts once more; once more the Holy Spirit makes his temple in us, and from the temple flow streams of living water—grace that irrigates our hardened souls and fertilizes them anew. Now is the time to sow in our hearts the heavenly Grain that will spring up in us and bring forth the fruit of justice—what other Grain than the divine principle of supernatural life which is imparted to us in Holy Communion?

THIRD POINT. *The Sacrament of Love.* But the Sacrament is more than this; like the ladder of Jacob that reached from earth to heaven, it is the actual meeting-place of God's chosen people with himself. To the heathen he gave the instinct of offering sacrifice and of desiring sacramental union, with no means, as yet, of satisfying it. To the Jews he gave temporary ordinances that were the types of sacraments to come, yet were in themselves unavailing. What other nation is there, then, so great as the Christian nation, that has its God drawing near to it? With what grateful love ought we to acknowledge this supreme privilege, of seeing him, who will one day sit in judgment on the whole of mankind, truly present on our altars, at once concealed and revealed under earthly forms, and throned in the monstrance!

I said, I will take heed to my ways, that I sin not with my tongue ;

I have set a guard to my mouth while the sinner stood against me. I was dumb, and was humbled, and kept silence from good things, and my sorrow was renewed.

My heart grew hot within me, and in my meditation a fire shall flame out.

I spoke with my tongue, O Lord, make me know my end, and what is the number of my days, that I may know what is wanting to me.

Behold, thou hast made my days measurable, and my substance is as nothing before thee.

The two great tests of love are readiness for sacrifice and desire for intimacy; and behold! He who was sacrificed for our sins here vouchsafes to make himself known to us, delighting to be with the sons of men.

Acts : Charity towards all men, loyalty to the Church, desire for more abundant life, love and gratitude to the Saviour who thus invites our intimacy.

Colloquy with Jesus as our King, our Life, and our Friend.

14. Ps. XXXVIII. (Dixi, custodiam).
RIGHT DISPOSITIONS IN LOSS OR BEREAVEMENT.

FIRST POINT. *Not only the tongue, but the heart, must refrain from murmuring against Providence.* It is something if we have learned not to murmur openly in times of distress, by complaining against Providence and courting human sympathy. This is a matter we should be all the more careful about when we are in the presence of such as neglect God, for in that case murmuring causes scandal, as well as being a sin. But, this grace once given us, how hard it is not to relieve, in secret, the pent-up distress of our minds, by outbursts of self-commiseration and recrimination with God! With this bereavement, this loss, this humiliation behind us, what are we to make of the span of life God has left us? Is it worth while to try and build up the shattered life anew; or is the time too short, and had we better creep to the grave in bitterness of soul? God remains silent, although he knows precisely the circumstances of our future : does he care at all, or is the fortune of one soul a matter of indifference to him?

And behold, all things are vanity, every man living.

Surely man passeth as an image; yea, and he is disquieted in vain.

He storeth up, and he knows not for whom he shall gather these things.

And now what is my hope? Is it not the Lord?
And my substance is with thee.

Deliver me from all my iniquities; thou hast made me a reproach to the fool.
I was dumb, and I opened not my mouth, because thou hast done it.

Remove thy scourges from me. The strength of thy hand hath made me faint in rebukes; thou hast corrected man for iniquity.

And thou hast made his soul to waste away like a spider: surely in vain is any man disquieted.

SECOND POINT. *We must learn our own littleness if we are to acquire such patience as that.* It is the fact that the fortunes, not merely of one soul but of the whole human race, are vanity when compared with God : they can add nothing to his essential glory. And it is the fact that, in the light of eternity, man's life is but for a moment, like a dream just before we awake from sleep. Man's feverish efforts to gain reputation, or to collect riches, are efforts vainly bestowed : the fame is lost and its echoes die away amid the noise of later reputations, and the riches pass, almost as soon as they are acquired, into the hands of an heir who may misuse or dissipate them. What hope then is left to man ? Only the hope of being united to God and enjoying him for ever. What reality remains amid the flux of mortal things ? Only the eternal value which each soul has in the sight of God's Providence. Measured by this standard, our sins and imperfections are follies that a child might laugh at. Be dumb, my soul ; cease from these impertinent murmurings ; the Lord gave and the Lord has taken away ; he has smitten and only he can save.

THIRD POINT. *Our prayer should be only that we may not give way to despair.* Humiliation is good for us, inasmuch as it reminds us of our sins, corrects their effects, and in part atones for them. It must not be allowed to break our spirits. The ambitions we so prized, the hopes we had so lovingly formed, have vanished from us like a torn spider's web, vain efforts, like all the efforts of man. But our tears must not be the tears of petulance and despair ; rather the tears of penitence, that will call down a renewal of God's favours. He

Hear my prayer, O Lord, and my supplication; give ear to my tears: be not silent, for I am a stranger with thee, and a sojourner as all my fathers were.

O forgive me, that I may be refreshed, before I go hence, and be no more.

When I called upon him, the God of my justice heard me; when I was in distress, thou hast enlarged me. Have mercy on me, and hear my prayer.

O ye sons of men, how long will you be dull of heart?

Why do you love vanity,

and seek after lying?

Know ye also that the Lord hath made his holy one wonderful; the Lord will hear me when I shall cry to him.

has not become deaf to our prayers ; he does but pity us the more, because we are only pilgrims on earth, strangers that remain but for a day in a country not ours. He will give us times of refreshment, and restore the wasted fibres of the soul : only let us learn to make the rest of our lives a right preparation for eternity.

Acts : Resignation, sense of our own nothingness, resolution against the sin of despair.

Colloquy with our Creator upon the use of the years that remain to us.

15. Ps. IV. (Cum invocarem).

YIELDING TO DEPRESSION IS FAITHLESSNESS TO GOD.

FIRST POINT. *We must not hasten to seek worldly consolations in trouble.* How many of those who say they find no consolation in religion would have to admit, if they examined their hearts, that in time of trouble they habitually forget to call upon God. Yet how else, when troubles beset us round, should we expect to find a way made clear for our feet, a breathing-space given us ? It is because, and in so far as, we are sons of the world that we allow our hearts to grow listless and dull, abandoning even our usual feeble efforts at prayer whenever we find that the weight of our depression indisposes us. Some plunge into unnecessary pleasures and relaxations, as if these ephemeral toys could rid us of the evil spirit ; some complain of their woes and exaggerate them, in the attempt to capture sympathy from their friends—sympathy easily expressed, but little felt. Yet when we read in the stories of the Saints how God mysteriously

E

Be ye angry, and sin not ;

the things you say in your hearts, be sorry for them upon your beds.

Offer up the sacrifice of justice,

and trust in the Lord.
Many say, Who sheweth us good things ?

The light of thy countenance, O Lord, is signed upon us, thou hast given gladness in my heart.

comforted them in spiritual desolations unimaginable to our earth-bound minds, should we not be well advised to seek, in our own measure, comfort from the same Source ?

SECOND POINT. *Deliberate pessimism is a sin against hope.* " Be ye angry, and sin not "—a difficult expression which St. Paul (*Eph.* iv. 26) seems to explain by adding " Let not the sun go down upon your anger." Angry feelings, sometimes of justifiable indignation, are practically unavoidable ; sin only comes in when we nurse our grievances, exaggerate them by continually turning them over in our minds, like a man deliberately keeping his wounds open. These murmurings, even if not inflicted on others but merely allowed to rankle in our hearts, are sins which we should confess to God and clear them off our conscience before we go to sleep at night. In so far as our tribulations are not directly the result of wrong-doing on our part, we can make an offering of them and of our innocence to God : thus they become a source of merit instead of sin. Confidence in God is not a mere support to fall back on if we will ; it is a Christian duty. Yet how many allow themselves to be discouraged even by small afflictions, and (at least for a time) take an altogether jaundiced view of life, thinking the whole world out of joint merely because they have some petty grievance !

THIRD POINT. *As Christians, let us take refuge in Christian consolations.* As Christians, we have been marked in Baptism with the sign of our divine deliverance ; God means us to find happiness only by having our soul's regard centred on

By the fruit of their corn, their wine, and oil, they are multiplied.

In peace in the selfsame I will sleep and I will rest,

for thou, O Lord, singularly hast settled me in hope.

I will bless the Lord at all times; his praise shall be always in my mouth.

In the Lord shall my soul be praised; let the meek hear and rejoice.

him, not on the world. The food by which Christians are fortified against the accidents of mortality is not worldly dissipation, but the secret operation of God's grace in the Sacrament of his Body and Blood ; the salve which is to make us invulnerable against the darts of the enemy is not human comfort, but the grace conferred on us by the Holy Spirit when we were anointed at Confirmation. Let us then take our rest quietly, in spite of distractions ; in peace, the peace of God which passes all understanding ; " in the self-same " (*in id ipsum*), that is, like a city invincible from without because it enjoys tranquillity within. How much scandal it must give that Christians, bidden to look forward to the eternal happiness of heaven, should be disconcerted by every breath of temporal affliction !

Acts : Confidence in God ; oblation to him of our earthly disquietudes.

Colloquy with the Sacred Heart, " source of all consolation."

16. Ps. XXXIII. (Benedicam Dominum).

CONSIDERATIONS ON DELIVERANCE FROM TROUBLE.

FIRST POINT. *The soul, delivered from troubles, would have all the world rejoice with it.* Hitherto I have often neglected to bless and praise God ; now, by his help, I mean to make the rest of my life a continuous offering of praise to him. Now and henceforward I will ascribe to God all the glory which self-love bids me take to myself ; I will join myself to the number of those meek souls, who have learned to distrust themselves, whether Saints in heaven or still alive on the earth ; I unite my

O magnify the Lord with me, and let us extol his Name together. I sought the Lord, and he heard me, and he delivered me from all my troubles.

Come ye to him, and be enlightened,

and your faces shall not be confounded.

This poor man cried, and the Lord heard him, and saved him out of all his troubles.

The angel of the Lord shall encamp round about them that fear him, and shall deliver them.

O taste and see that the Lord is sweet; blessed is the man that hopeth in him.

Fear the Lord, all ye his saints, for there is no want to them that fear him.

The rich have wanted, and have suffered hunger, but they that seek the Lord shall not be deprived of any good.

Come, children, hearken to me; I will teach you the fear of the Lord. Who is the man that desireth life?

intention with theirs in extolling God's holy Name. I turned in my trouble to look for God, and found him close at hand to deliver me. Would that all men might have recourse to him, and experience the illumination—that is, the guidance and the hope—which he is ready to give ; unfailingly ready, so that no one need fear disappointment and embarrassment through having applied to him in vain. What was I when I cried and found deliverance ? I was poor—that is, I was destitute of earthly help, and destitute at the same time of all merit, all claim upon his goodness. I was poor—that is, I recognized my own nothingness and helplessness, and to such souls God is merciful. They have, all unseen, the arms of their guardian angel stretched round them, like a friendly host encamped about them on their pilgrimage.

SECOND POINT. *The blessedness of serving God in itself counterweighs our earthly troubles.* The soul that has really tasted the intimacy of God derives from it a sweetness which is undisturbed by earthly circumstance. The soul that has seriously considered God's greatness, and learned to fear him, will not be dismayed by merely temporal needs. It is those who think themselves rich—that is, those who are self-satisfied and worldly, without consciousness of spiritual need—who are really poor, for the riches, the human support, the temporal advantages which they cherish are in themselves unreal, and desert them in time of trouble ; those who make God the end of their striving will never be baffled in their search. This, then, is the secret of the God-fearing soul. You want life? The sense of free, untrammelled action, of exercising your powers to the full ? You want

Who loveth to see good days?

Keep thy tongue from evil,
and thy lips from speaking guile.

Turn away from evil, and do good;

seek peace and pursue it.

The eyes of the Lord are upon the just, and his ears unto their prayers; but the countenance of the Lord is against them that do evil, to cut off the remembrance of them from the earth.

The just cried, and the Lord heard them, and delivered them out of all their troubles;

The Lord is nigh unto them that are of a contrite heart, and he will save the humble of spirit.

Many are the afflictions of the just, but out of them all will the Lord deliver them: the Lord keepeth all their bones; not one of them shall be broken.

The death of the wicked is very evil, and they that hate the just shall be guilty: the Lord will redeem the souls of his servants, and none of them that trust in him shall offend.

" good days "—not short, violent sensations of pleasure, but steady, enduring happiness ? Then you must mortify your desire to criticize, to back-bite, to complain ; you must cultivate honesty and frankness of speech—so many of our miseries come from misuse of the tongue. You must learn to love good and hate evil as you see it around you ; you must learn to live peaceably with men, and to love silence and recollection. If you are thus mortified, half your troubles disappear, and the other half became lighter to bear.

THIRD POINT. *But, beyond this, God does specially preserve the soul that seeks him, if not from all trouble, at least from the sins trouble tempts us to.* God sees, hears, knows, everything that goes on in the world, but with this difference—he has a kindly eye and an attentive ear for the just ; the unjust have only the reprobation of his frown. Although he will not buy human love by automatically (as it were) rewarding goodness, he does shew special temporal mercies to his own ; and more especially when he sees that trouble has already had the effect of humbling them and producing contrition. Even so we must not expect to escape the afflictions by which God tests us here ; all he guarantees is that in his hands we can suffer no vital injury, *i.e.*, no harm affecting the inward life of the soul : unlike the worldly, the just escape the terrors of an unrepentant deathbed, and of eternal guilt ; they are redeemed from the power of their spiritual enemy, and trouble itself cannot lead them into sin and despair.

Acts : Thanksgiving, with determination to show our gratitude in our lives ; detachment from the world ; confidence in God's protection.

Colloquy with God who invites you to be enlightened and to taste his sweetness.

With-expectation I have waited for the Lord,
and he was attentive to me.

And he heard my prayers, and brought me
out of the pit of misery and out of the mire of
dregs.
And he set my feet upon a rock.
and directed my steps.

Many shall see and fear, and they shall hope
in the Lord: blessed is the man whose trust
is in the Lord, and who hath not had regard to
vanities and lying follies.

Thou hast multiplied thy wonderful works,
O Lord my God, and in thy thoughts there is
no one like unto thee:
I have declared and I have spoken; they are
multiplied above number.

Sacrifice and oblation thou didst not desire,
but thou hast pierced ears for me.

Burnt-offering and sin-offering thou didst
not require;

17. Ps. XXXIX. (Expectans expectavi).

A GREAT TEMPORAL DELIVERANCE.

FIRST POINT. *Acknowledgment of God's mercy.*
How full of consolation it is, after deliverance,
to remember the long, weary time of waiting,
during which God tested our patience and exercised us in prayer ! It seemed, then, as if our feet
were set on a quagmire, and every step we took
forward plunged us yet deeper in the morass that
threatened to suck us down ; now, as if in a
moment, we have felt the firm rock beneath us,
with its easy footholds ; and once again the way
seems clearly marked in front of us, so that we
shall not easily lose our path again. Oh that
those who have never experienced the agonies
and the power of prayer might now share our
feelings ; that they might learn to derive hope and
consolation from God, instead of vainly seeking
comfort and relaxation in his transitory creatures !
We do not know whether to admire more the Power
which has delivered us, or the Wisdom which has
allowed us to be thus exercised ; our comprehension
is baffled alike by the vastness of the one and by
the depth of the other.

SECOND POINT. *God, who has spared us the
sacrifice of loss, can demand all the more imperatively
the sacrifice of the will.* And yet, had it been God's
will that we should drain the bitterness to its dregs
and pass the rest of our life without respite or relief,
how gladly ought we to have resigned ourselves
to such a lot, offering our troubles as a holocaust
to his glory ! He has not seen fit to demand this
of us. It is the same God who demanded of
Abraham the sacrifice of his only son Isaac, and

then said I, Behold, I come.

In the head of the book it is written of me that I should do thy will; O my God, I have desired it, and thy law in the midst of my heart.

I have desired thy justice in a great church; lo, I will not restrain my lips; O Lord, thou knowest it. I have not hid thy justice within my heart, I have declared thy truth and thy salvation. I have not concealed thy mercy and truth from a great council.

Withhold not then, O Lord, thy tender mercies from me; thy mercy and thy truth have always upheld me.

For evils without number have surrounded me; my iniquities have overtaken me, and I was not able to see.

They are multiplied above the hairs of my head, and my heart hath forsaken me.

Be pleased, O Lord, to deliver me; look down, O Lord, to help me.

Let them be confounded and ashamed together, that seek after my soul to take it away: let them be turned backward and ashamed that desire evils to me. Let them immediately bear their confusion, that say to me, 'Tis well, 'tis well.

then reprieved him at the last moment in reward for his obedience. In our case, too, God has accepted our willingness to suffer instead of our actual suffering; it is the obedience he prizes, the spirit that says " Lo ! I come." Now, in the time of my distress, I have resigned myself completely into his hands : my vow is registered in heaven. I must keep this vow by labouring to imprint his image ever more firmly on my heart; I must make it my business to console others, and to help them, as prudence allows, to the recognition of the faith which has stood me in such good stead : I must be ever ready to vindicate to others God's justice, the truth of his revelation, and the width of his mercies.

THIRD POINT. *My spiritual dangers still remain, and I must always beg for the same deliverance from them.* The mercy and faithfulness of God, which have been made known to me in this temporal deliverance, will not desert me when I ask for spiritual favours. The case of my soul, but for his grace, is even more desperate than were my fortunes a little while ago—if only I had power to see it ; but the very multitude of my sins blinds me to their heinousness. When I think seriously of my many imperfections, my heart fails within me. May he, here too, take pity on me, and set my feet firmly on the rock of His salvation. My spiritual enemies hope, no doubt, that this deliverance will lead me into the sin of pride, ingratitude, or presumption ; so many souls err in this way that they might well count me an easy prey. Grant, Lord, that my heart may always overflow with gratitude for this and for all thy mercies to men : grant that I may ever remember what I am,

Let all that seek thee rejoice and be glad in thee, and let such as love thy salvation say always, The Lord be magnified.

But I am a beggar and poor; the Lord is careful for me. Thou art my helper and my protector; O my God, be not slack.

Preserve me, O Lord, for I have put my trust in thee. I have said to the Lord, Thou art my God, for thou hast no need of my goods.

To the saints, who are in his land, he hath made wonderful all my desires in them.

Their infirmities were multiplied : afterwards they made haste.

a creature destitute of spiritual resources, now and
always a pensioner on thy grace.   Yet I can never
ask too often ; thou carest for me, and wilt not
be slow to answer though I should appeal again
and again for deliverance.

Acts : Gratitude, complete dedication of our
wills, confidence.

Colloquy with God as our rescuer from a morass
of danger.

18. Ps. XV. (Conserva me Domine).
GOD'S BLESSINGS IN TIME AND ETERNITY.

FIRST POINT. *God " does not need either man's
work or his own gifts."*   Thou art my God, *because*
thou hast no need of my goods. To everything
else that is called mine,—*my* King, *my* country,
my family, etc.—I can contribute something which
completes their happiness or well-being :   only
my God is *mine* in a sense which gives me no
proprietorship whatever.   All the blessings I have
are his gift, and even when I use them to his praise
I only add to his glory accidentally, not substanti-
ally, for he is in all things self-sufficing.   Hence
my spiritual ambitions must be formed upon the
wonderful model he has given me in the *Saints*
who now enjoy our heavenly country.   " Their
infirmities were multiplied ;   afterwards they
made haste "—or, as St. Paul tells us, they " re-
covered strength from weakness."   Saint Peter
learns what it is to fall ; Saint Paul is afflicted
with an infirmity of the flesh ; the great mystics
pass, for a time, through a period of spiritual
dryness, *in order to give them distrust of themselves* ; when God's grace intervenes later, see

I will not gather together their meetings for blood,

nor will I be mindful of their names by my lips.

The Lord is the portion of my inheritance and of my cup; it is thou that wilt restore my inheritance to me.

The lines are fallen unto me in goodly places : for my inheritance is goodly to me.

I will bless the Lord, who hath given me understanding : my reins also have corrected me even till night.

I set the Lord always in my sight : for he is at my right hand, that I be not moved.

Therefore my heart hath been glad, and my tongue hath rejoiced ;

moreover my flesh also shall rest in hope.

how easily they acquire the virtues and rise to perfection !

SECOND POINT. *The devout soul, turning away from the world, is enriched with great spiritual blessings, but even these must not exalt us, or make us forget our continual dependence* " Their meetings " : when he said " Thou art my God," the sacred writer was thinking of the false gods worshipped by others, and to these he suddenly turns. I must not immerse myself in the society of worldly people, who in their practice worship Nature instead of God ; I must not let my mind dwell too much on earthly cares : God himself is the portion of my inheritance and of my cup (*i.e.* destiny) ; He " restores " my inheritance when He compensates by His grace for the gifts I have lost through Adam's transgression. (For clerics this verse will have a special meaning.) And what an inheritance ! God for my Father, the Church for my home, the Sacrament for my food, the Saints for my companions, etc. But blessed is he to whom God gives prudence in the use of this happiness, whose conscience reminds him, from morning to night, of the dangers it entails, such as giving way to pride or falling short of grace. Such a man puts God always before him, as the end and aim of all his actions, and feels God " on his right hand " knowing that his grace is the support which saves even the best of us from falling.

THIRD POINT. *In any case, the fulness of spiritual blessings is to be enjoyed only in Heaven.*

The blessings God bestows on me even now, both temporal and spiritual, should be enough to make me cry out in gratitude ; but he does more, and gives me a hope beyond the grave. As he

Because thou wilt not leave my soul in hell ;
nor wilt thou give thy holy one to see corruption.

Thou hast made known to me the ways of
life ;

thou shalt fill me with joy with thy countenance :

at thy right hand are delights even to the end.

Lord, thou hast been our refuge from generation to generation.

Before the mountains were made, or the
earth and the world was formed, from eternity
and to eternity thou art God.

Turn not man away to be brought low.
And thou hast said, Be converted, O ye sons of
men.

For a thousand years in thy sight are as
yesterday, which is past,

raised up the human Soul of Jesus from the place
of departed spirits, and his Body from the tomb,
so he promises to raise up our bodies at the Last
Day, and to bring our souls out of Purgatory to
the enjoyment of heaven.   Thus his revelation lets
us into the secret of eternal life ; and, little though
we can imagine our future blessedness, we know :

(i) that the spiritual sight of God will fill us
with happiness in a measure we have never dreamed
of here, the mere happiness of contemplation ;

(ii) that " at his right hand," *i.e.* among the
elect souls (*Matthew* xxv. 33) there are other delights
endless both in their measure and their duration.

Acts : Distrust of your own strength, dedication
of all our blessings to God, aspiration to the joys
of Heaven.

Colloquy of gratitude to God for his principal
blessings in your own life.

19.   Ps. LXXXIX. (Domine refugium).

THE SHORTNESS OF LIFE.

FIRST POINT. *Our life compared with God's
eternity.*   In the troubles and distractions of our
earthly life, there is one thought that should be constantly near, either to console or to control us—the
eternity of God. His existence, itself altogether
outside of and unconditioned by time, recedes
infinitely (in our human mode of calculation)
into the past and into the future. To let the
imagination feed on this truth has, at first, the
effect of altogether crushing our spirits and fright-
ening us away ; this is not the effect God intends.
If we will think of the meaning of our life in the
light of God's eternity, it will be a sure way to

And as a watch in the night, things that are counted nothing, shall their years be. In the morning man shall grow up like grass; in the morning he shall flourish and pass away: in the evening he shall fall, grow dry, and wither.

For in thy wrath we have fainted away, and are troubled in thy indignation.

Thou hast set our iniquities before thy eyes, our life in the light of thy countenance.

For all our days are spent, and in thy wrath we have fainted away.

Our years shall be considered as a spider; the days of our years in them are threescore and ten years: but if in the strong they be fourscore years, and what is more of them is labour and sorrow.

For mildness is come upon us, and we shall be corrected.

Who knoweth the power of thy anger, and for thy fear can number thy wrath?

So make thy right hand known, and men learned in heart, in wisdom.

conversion of the heart. With him, a thousand years are as one day, a mere brief episode : nay, time itself is lost in an eternal Now. In His sight a human life is simply the turn of a watchman at his post ; maturity follows upon youth, and decay upon maturity so soon, that the brief time of man's probation loses all value and colour of its own, and is seen merely as a preparation for eternity.

SECOND POINT. *Sin in the light of eternity.* And that preparation—how miserably used ! How little we should shrink from God's chastisements in time, if we could always remember that he has our eternal destiny in view ! Our sins, even when we ourselves are unconscious of their weight, lie open and naked in his sight ; our worldliness is seen in its true colours in that infallible Light in which God sees the hearts of men. Our allotted days slip away from us almost unnoticed ; almost unnoticed, too, the offences against God which mount up as our life goes on : are declining years to bring a better mind ? Or are we to risk an eternity of God's displeasure ? And that in exchange for something as frail and unsubstantial as a spider's web,—the enjoyment of our brief human existence ; seventy or eighty years, perhaps, and how many of them darkened by infirmities, miseries, anxieties, and despairs ? God's mercy inflicts these upon us, precisely lest we should forget, in unchequered happiness, the small worth of our life here. Otherwise, so weak are we, it would be hard for us to keep in mind the claims God has upon us, and avert his anger by the constant exercise of holy fear. O may His hand never cease to visit us with chastisement, until we have learned that divine wisdom which consists

Return, O Lord: how long? And be entreated in favour of thy servants.

We are filled in the morning with thy mercy, and we have rejoiced and are delighted all our days.

We have rejoiced for the days in which thou hast humbled us; for the years in which we have seen evils.

Look upon thy servants and upon their works, and direct their children.

And let the brightness of the Lord our God be upon us, and direct thou the work of our hands over us; yea, the work of our hands do thou direct.

Hear these things, all ye nations; give ear, all ye inhabitants of the world: all you that are earth-born, and you sons of men, both rich and poor together.

in a proper disposition of our hearts towards him !

THIRD POINT. *Renewal of resolutions.* How long will it be before God will give us grace to live simply for his service ? Would that this very morning might see the dawn in our souls of that heavenly illumination, which alone can bring true happiness in a miserable world ! True happiness, because the possession of it enables us to see, in all our humiliations and adversities, the correction of our faults and (please God) some remission of our time in Purgatory. We are the creatures of his hand, bound to him by an infinite debt of service ; may he teach us, then, to direct all our works to the sole intention of his glory : may the consciousness of his enlightening presence be with us continually, so that, as far as possible, no moment of our transitory lives may be wasted by being spent on occupations which we cannot devote to his honour.

Acts : Adoration of God's eternity ; fear of our judgment ; resolution to devote our works to God.

Colloquy with God who foresees our life and our last end.

20. Ps. XLVIII. (Audite haec).
DEATH.

FIRST POINT. *Death the inevitable lot of all.* The warning which death brings to us is one of the motives of natural religion, appealing as much to the heathen as to the Christian ; striking a chill even into the most earthly-minded of our fellow-men, not affected in its seriousness by the affluence or the poverty of their worldly conditions. Yet

My mouth shall speak wisdom, and the meditation of my heart understanding : I will incline my ear to a parable, I will open my proposition on the psaltery.

Why shall I fear in the evil day ? The iniquity of my heel shall encompass me. They that trust in their own strength, and glory in the multitude of their riches.

No brother can redeem, nor shall man redeem ; he shall not give to God his ransom, nor the price of the redemption of his soul, and shall labour for ever, and shall still live unto the end.

He shall not see destruction, when he shall see the wise dying ; the senseless and the fool shall perish together,

and they shall leave their riches to strangers, and their sepulchres shall be their houses for ever,

Their dwelling-places to all generations. They have called their lands by their names.

And man when he was in honour did not understand ; he is compared to senseless beasts, and is become like to them.

This way of theirs is a stumbling-block to them, and afterwards they shall delight in their mouth.

it is the part of wisdom to meditate frequently and deeply on a fact so obvious, because of the light it throws on the way in which our life should be lived. It is easy for the rich and powerful to think that they have secured themselves against the blows of adversity, and that the unscrupulous means by which they have amassed their fortune will insure them against losing it. But there comes a time when their own strength of necessity fails them, and their riches can avail them no more ; no family influence, no highly-placed friends can protect them from the dreadful summons of Almighty God, or give them freedom to live on through the centuries, still devoted to their worldly ambitions.

SECOND POINT. *Nevertheless, the worldly remain indifferent to God.* The children of the world are too often unmoved by such thoughts ; they see others, far better prepared for death than themselves, taken from us ; yet they never seem to consider that, well or ill prepared, we must all be taken when our time comes ; that our worldly possessions must pass to others, and our tenement be a narrow strip of the cold ground. Is it not a mockery, then, that they should never think of death, while they are busied in building fine houses that will last long after them, and giving their names to the wooded lands whose trees they will never see coming to maturity ? For the dumb beasts, this careless attitude of living for the morrow is right and natural ; but man has been honoured with the special privilege of eternity, and a special duty of preparing for it :—how is it that he will not understand ? Alas, the very fact of their absorption in worldly projects, and their

They are laid in hell like sheep; death shall feed upon them, and the just shall have dominion over them in the morning; and their help shall decay in hell from their glory.

But God will redeem my soul from the hand of hell, when he shall receive me.

Be not thou afraid, when a man shall be made rich, and when the glory of his house shall be increased; for when he shall die he shall take nothing away, nor shall his glory descend with him.

For in his life-time his soul will be blessed, and he will praise thee when thou shalt do well to him: he shall go in to the generations of his fathers, and he shall never see light.

Man when he was in honour did not understand; he hath been compared to senseless beasts, and made like to them.

The Lord said to my Lord,

self-congratulation on worldly prosperity, is the snare that ruins such souls ; in death they will be tongue-tied before the terrible justice of God ; and when the righteous awake glorious in the Kingdom of their Father, the children of the world will find all help far off, and all their glory faded.

THIRD POINT. *Let us learn to practise a holy indifference to the world.* But we, who have learned to devote ourselves to the acquiring of spiritual resources, will find treasure in that day—the precious Blood of our Redeemer, whereby we are made acceptable to God. How then can we allow ourselves to be anxious and ambitious over the bestowal of earthly goods, which, like the name and fame which so often goes with them, cannot help us against our needs in eternity ? We will not envy the position of those who enjoy all their happiness in this world, and give thanks for none but temporal blessings, and forget that when they are gathered to their fathers their best prayer will be to be delivered from the darkness of Purgatory into the eternal light of Heaven. O my soul, we have been honoured above the beasts of the field by being created for an eternal destiny : shall we not be wise in time to attain it ?

Acts : Fear of God's judgments ; detachment ; resignation.

Colloquy with God as our only End.

21. Ps. CIX. (Dixit Dominus Domino meo).
CHRISTMAS DAY.

FIRST POINT. *The Hypostatic Union.* God is, by his title of creation, the Lord of all things ; but, for the sake of fallen Man, he has earned afresh

Sit thou at my right hand,

Until I make thy enemies thy footstool.

The Lord will send forth the sceptre of thy power out of Sion ;

Rule thou in the midst of thy enemies.

With thee is the principality in the day of thy strength, in the brightness of the Saints :

From the womb before the day-star I begot thee.

the title of "our Lord" by a more personal and intimate claim. There has been no time in history when the Divine Word was not seated at the Father's right Hand, enjoying the full prerogatives of the Godhead. Yet, at a point in time, the Divine Word did condescend to take upon Him our flesh, that in the likeness of sinful man he might overthrow the dominion of the devil brought about by man's sin. He is born of Juda, a member of the race that has been mysteriously set apart and prepared by God for the preservation of the true religion and for the advent of the Redeemer. Yet he comes to his own, and his own do not receive him. The Kingdom he comes to found is one which is to do continual battle amidst a world of sin ; so he, its Founder, takes upon himself not merely a Human Nature but a despised and persecuted Human Nature, a sign everywhere spoken against.

Second Point. *The Virgin birth.* See how, at the mere whisper of Christ's coming, his glory already begins to manifest itself in his chosen Saints : how John is miraculously born, Mary favoured with a heavenly visit ; how the Forerunner, while yet in the womb, greets her who carries in her Womb the Lamb of God : how the holy Angels and the stars themselves cannot keep the secret, but proclaim it to the shepherds and the Kings, that they may come and adore. But the chief and the most central miracle of all is the conception of Christ by the operation of the Holy Spirit in the Womb of his immaculate Mother, and her virgin child-bearing. So Christ comes secretly where he is least expected ; comes, too, at midnight, when silence holds all around,

The Lord hath sworn, and will not repent:
Thou art a priest for ever according to the
order of Melchisedech.

The Lord at thy right hand hath broken
Kings in the day of his wrath.

He shall judge among nations :

He shall fill ruins,

He shall crush the heads in the land of many.
He shall drink of the torrent in the way ;

Therefore shall he lift up the head.

with all the circumstances of sanctity and of privacy due to such an Advent. For he who comes is " without father and without mother, having neither beginning of days nor end of life " ; though truly Man, he is not brought into being at this birth, but has been from all eternity, begotten before the worlds by a mysterious Generation in the bosom of the Godhead.

THIRD POINT. *The Kingdom of Christ.* And hardly is the Child born, before he has to be rescued by a wonderful Providence from the treacherous cruelty of an earthly king. Involuntarily, the wicked tyrant does tribute to the Kingship of Christ that has been revealed to the Wise Men. He is a King indeed, who is to judge and find wanting his ancient people, the Jews, and, disappointed of faith here, is to build up on the ruins of the old dispensation a new People, chosen from every nation under heaven : in that Kingdom, as he tells us, many that are last will be first, and the first last. Yet he does not come in the Kingly state that befits his divine Majesty, but as a *viator*, as Man in his state of humiliation, depending for his sustenance and preservation on the common resources of humanity : it is only in virtue of that humiliation that he is to receive, in his glorified human Nature, the Name that is above every name, that at the Name of Jesus, the little Child born in Bethlehem, every knee in Heaven and earth should bow.

Acts : Adoration of this great mystery ; congratulation with the Blessed Virgin ; humility in union with the humiliation of Christ.

Colloquy with the uncrowned King who comes to · visit his own.

Give to the King thy judgment, O God, and to the King's son thy justice, to judge thy people with justice, and thy poor with judgment. Let the mountains receive peace for the people, and the hills justice. He shall judge the poor of the people, and he shall save the children of the poor, and he shall humble the oppressor.

And he shall continue with the sun and before the moon, throughout all generations.

He shall come down like the rain upon the fleece, and as showers falling gently upon the earth.

In his days shall justice spring up, and abundance of peace, till the moon be taken away; and he shall rule from sea to sea, and from the river unto the ends of the earth.

Before him the Ethiopians shall fall down, and his enemies shall lick the ground: the Kings of Tharsis and the isles shall offer presents; the Kings of the Arabians and of Saba shall bring gifts.

And all kings of the earth shall adore him, all nations shall serve him; for he shall deliver the poor from the mighty, and the needy that

22. Ps. LXXI. (Deus judicium).
THE EPIPHANY.

FIRST POINT. *Permanence of the Kingdom of Christ.* Solomon, the son of the war-like king David, was enabled by God to enhance the prosperity and size of his kingdom by justice and by peaceful means ; this psalm refers to him, and applies naturally to the peaceful kingdom of the Child whom the kings of the East came to worship. The Kingdom of Christ is distinguished from the ambitious dynasties of the world at once by the all-seeing justice of its Sovereign and by the bloodless weapons of its warfare. Its spiritual privileges are offered to rich and poor alike ; nay, in it the poor are even congratulated on their humble station. While thrones totter, the Kingdom of God is indestructible, and must endure till the consummation of all things. See how secretly this King comes to his own, whether in the stable at Bethlehem or in the depths of the human heart, like the silent drops of rain that gradually flood all around them ! Yet the Wise Kings are right in offering their tribute ; for, when the very fame of their empires has passed away, the new Kingdom of Justice and Peace will continue to enlarge its borders.

SECOND POINT. *Universality of the Kingdom of Christ.* Christ's Kingdom is universal in its outward extent ; for all their differences of race and temperament, it is designed for the barbarous Ethiopian, the cultivated traders of the Mediterranean, the ancient civilizations of the East, as much as for the Jew. It is universal in its application to the conditions of society, calling for the homage of the highest and elevating the dignity

G

had no helper. He shall spare the poor and needy, and he shall save the souls of the poor; he shall redeem their souls from usuries and iniquity, and their names shall be honourable in his sight.

And he shall live, and to him shall be given of the gold of Arabia; for him they shall always adore, they shall bless him all the day.

And there shall be a firmament on the earth on the tops of the mountains; above Libanus shall the fruit thereof be exalted, and they of the city shall flourish like the grass of the earth.

Let his name be blessed for evermore; his name continueth before the sun;

and in him shall all the tribes of the earth be blessed; all nations shall magnify him.

Blessed be the Lord, the God of Israel, who alone doth wonderful things, and blessed be the name of his majesty for ever, and the whole earth shall be filled with his majesty. So be it. So be it.

of the lowest in the world's estimation ; the Church is to be the conscience of nations, and see that the most defenceless of her children do not suffer wrong while she can make an effective protest. It is universal also in the claim it makes upon our lives : in the days of Solomon, we are told, silver was reckoned as of almost no value, so great was the influx of gold into the Kingdom, and the Kingdom of Christ puts to shame our second-bests and our protestations that " this will do" by continually demanding our whole selves and all we have, so that there is no height of sanctity at which we can say "This is enough: God is satisfied."

THIRD POINT. *Blessings of the Kingdom of Christ.* The Church, with her deposit of truth and her inheritance of the Sacraments, is a divine source of strength in the midst of the world, exalted above all human institutions. The spiritual blessings entrusted to her keeping are worth more than all the riches of creation ; yet, instead of being jealously hoarded, they are squandered in magnificent profusion on us her children, so ungrateful, so unworthy. As the sun distributes its light and heat to all mankind, so the Child whose dawning glories are already reflected in the soul of his Immaculate Mother comes to illuminate all minds and to kindle all hearts ; he comes to sanctify to his own use the special gifts and the special genius of every nation under heaven. Let us then, guided by the star of faith, come to worship the King thus miraculously born in human flesh : let us unite our hearts with the Divine Will that His Kingdom should endure triumphant to all time, and spread irresistibly to all corners of the earth.

The earth is the Lord's, and the fulness
thereof; the world, and all they that dwell
therein.

For he hath founded it upon the seas, and
prepared it upon the rivers.

Who shall ascend into the mountain of the
Lord, or who shall stand in his holy place?

Acts : Adoration of God Incarnate ; gratitude for the blessings given us through His Church.

Colloquy with the Holy Child, King of all hearts.

23. Ps. XXIII. (Domini est terra).
THE ASCENSION.

FIRST POINT. *Creation, and man as part of creation, belong to God.* The artist, who has given new form to a piece of matter, speaks of *his* work ; the father, who has endowed his son with physical life, but not with his soul, speaks of *his* son ; the proprietor of lands which, sooner or later, will pass from him to another, speaks of *his* lands. But in the full and proper sense nothing " belongs " except to God, the Artist who made both form and matter, the Father who gave us both physical and spiritual life, the King to whom the highest on earth must do fealty, as holding their possessions from him. God, as the original of all things, is their absolute possessor. But more ; he has founded his creation " on the seas," prepared it " upon the rivers " : that is, all that exists besides himself would, but for his continual act of conservation, perish and decay in a moment like a house built on a bog or a quicksand. He is, therefore, absolute Lord of all things not merely by the fact of their origin, but by the fact of their daily continuance.

SECOND POINT. *Hence the right use of the material creation is that which God enjoins on us, to rise above it.* This inferior creation, of which man has been given the mastery, has only been *lent* to him by God, and on one condition—that he should aspire to rise above it ; the end of man

The innocent in hands, and clean of heart,

who hath not taken his soul in vain,

nor sworn deceitfully to his neighbour.

He shall receive a blessing from the Lord, and mercy from God his Saviour. This is the generation of them that seek him, of them that seek the face of the God of Jacob.

Lift up your gates, O ye princes, and be ye lifted up, O eternal gates, and the King of Glory shall enter in. Who is this King of Glory? The Lord who is strong and mighty, the Lord mighty in battle. Lift up your gates, O ye princes, and be ye lifted up, O eternal gates, and the King of Glory shall enter in. Who is this King of Glory? The Lord of Hosts, he is the King of Glory.

is to attain to the vision of God and enjoy it eternally. Nature would have us revenge injuries, acquire goods unjustly, and so on ; or at least resent what we cannot revenge, covet what we cannot acquire : our eternal destiny requires of us that we should not merely avoid the sinful act, but purify our hearts from the bad intention. Nature encourages us to make light of the eternal issue that lies before our souls ; grace bids us make this our first care. Nature bids us keep on the right side of human opinion and respect ; God, who sees the heart, demands inward truth. Thus the bestowal of God's blessings, nay, even the remission of the punishments we so justly deserve, depend on the measure in which our hearts rise above the gift to the Giver, and dwell in heavenly places.

THIRD POINT. *Christ, our Head, by his Ascension into Heaven, has prepared the way to lead our souls upwards.* Christ storms the gates of heaven, bringing with Him the Sacred Humanity—the spoils He has rescued from a corrupt Nature and a fallen world. The Angels fall back and make room for a created Soul to pass into the bosom of the Godhead. He comes as Victor over hell and death ; in the seeming defeat of His Passion and the triumph of his Resurrection He has won for us, His faithful soldiers, the grace which will enable us to follow Him. We have still to fight on earth the battles of the Lord of Hosts, but the conquest is already achieved, and the centre of our affections has passed already from this treacherous world to the heavenly mansions He has prepared for us.

The Lord hath reigned, let the earth rejoice :
let many islands be glad.

Clouds and darkness are round about him ;
justice and judgment are the establishment of
his throne.

A fire shall go before him, and shall burn
his enemies round about ; his lightnings have
shone forth to the world ; the earth saw and
trembled.

The mountains melted like wax, at the presence of the Lord, at the presence of the Lord of
all the earth.

The heavens declared his justice, and all
people saw his glory.

Let them be all confounded that adore graven
things, and that glory in their idols.

Acts : Dependence upon God ; aspiration towards Heaven ; thanksgiving and praise for the glories of the Ascension.

Colloquy with Christ as our Captain who has gone before us.

24. Ps. XCVI. (Dominus regnavit, exultet).
THE HOLY ANGELS.

FIRST POINT. *The lower creation we know by sense speaks to us of that higher creation we know by faith.* The created world we live in seems, to the eye of faith, to be (as it were) bubbling over with a secret—the invisible majesty of the God who created it. How are we to try to picture something of His royal state ? Nature, in its grandeur, will help us. The mystery of the dark night and the overshadowing clouds speaks to us of that unutterable depth of wisdom in which, we are told, the Cherubim have a special share. The devouring rapacity of fire, and the alacrity with which, in the lightning, it speeds on its errand, remind us of that burning love which is typified to us in the Seraphim. The huge mountains, which are yet shaken by earthquakes or rent by volcanic eruptions, make us think of the mighty Forces above us that are yet subject to the will of God, the Dominations that adore and the Powers that tremble. And the thunder that shakes the heavens is an echo to earthly ears of the cry of praise that goes up to God, day and night, from his heavenly Court.

SECOND POINT. *This multiplication of created glories does not interfere with the unique Omnipotence of God.* We must not, however, think of the Divine Majesty as something shared with lesser

Adore him, all you his angels :   ·

Sion heard and was glad, and the daughters
of Juda rejoiced, because of thy judgments,
O Lord.
For thou art the most high Lord over all the
earth ; thou art exalted exceedingly above all
Gods.

You that love the Lord, hate evil : the Lord
preserveth the souls of his saints, he will deliver
them out of the hand of the sinner.

Light is risen to the just, and joy to the right
of heart.

Rejoice, ye just, in the Lord, and give praise
to the remembrance of his holiness.

beings, like the heathen who divided the single Nature of God into a whole hierarchy of deities who could rival, and even conflict with, one another. There is no power in heaven outside God himself which does not, merely because it is a creature, take rank infinitely below him, and confess the worship it owes to the one uncreated Being and Creator of all. This revelation that God is One was specially entrusted to the chosen people of Israel; it was the foundation of their laws and the secret of their invincible faith. God is infinitely high and infinitely holy; and all the conceptions of the divine Nature which the wisest philosophers have ever been able to form are wholly inadequate to express the uniqueness and transcendence of the idea they tried to convey.

THIRD POINT. *God sends his angels as guardians and as messengers to men.* It is well for us that our frail nature, so prone to relapse into sin, so loth to relinquish its attachment to vanities, is reinforced by the ministry of Angel Guardians in that battle with the Powers of Darkness which would otherwise go so hardly with us. But, more than all, the character of the holy Angels is made known to us by the occasions when they have been sent to make a revelation of God's will to man; and above all, in the visit of the Angel Gabriel to our blessed Lady, when Light came into the world, and the cause of all our joy. Let us then congratulate with the Holy Angels on the blessedness which is theirs—to serve God constantly and to dwell in his presence; and let us join with theirs our praises of the ineffable holiness of God, singing " Holy, Holy, Holy " in response to their heavenly anthem.

Praise the Lord, O my soul : in my life I will praise the Lord : I will sing to my God as long as I shall be.

Put not your trust in princes, in the children of men, in whom there is no salvation.

His spirit shall go forth, and he shall return into his earth; in that day shall all their thoughts perish.

Blessed is he who hath the God of Jacob for his helper, whose hope is in the Lord his God, who made heaven and earth, the sea, and all things that are in them.

Acts: Adoration of the unique Majesty of God ; congratulation with the Holy Angels ; gratitude for their ministry.

Colloquy with God exalted above every Power in heaven and earth.

25. Ps. CXLV. (Lauda, anima mea ... laudabo).

ALL SAINTS.

FIRST POINT. *Earthly compared with heavenly patronage.* How wise is he who, in this earthly life, makes it his first business to do honour, not to earthly dignities, but to God who is Lord both of this world and of the next ! It seems natural and profitable to make friends of those in high worldly position, and flatter ourselves on the number or the exalted station of our acquaintances. And yet those who so lay their plans may be defeated suddenly by the death of a powerful patron, who is scarcely laid in his coffin before his memory is forgotten and his policy reversed. And we, too, have death to face, and a judgment at which we must appear ; what safety shall we find then in great names and proud titles ? How we shall wish then that we had learnt to rely more on the chosen sons of God, the princes of his court, the patrons at his judgment seat—the blessed company of Saints !

SECOND POINT. *The Saints themselves centred their hopes in Heaven.* Truly we may call them blessed now, who did not regard at all the world's smiles and frowns, knowing that God was their protector. He, who in his omnipotence had made heaven and earth and sea, and in his omniscience had ordered, to the minutest detail, the furniture of

Who keepeth truth for ever ;
who executeth judgment for them that suffer
wrong ;

who giveth food to the hungry.

The Lord looseth them that are fettered ;

the Lord enlighteneth the blind.

The Lord lifteth up them that are cast down ;

the Lord loveth the just.

The Lord keepeth the strangers,

he will support the fatherless,
and the widow ;

and the ways of sinners he will destroy.

each—would he neglect them ? Would not the
Providence that cared for the sparrows protect the
interests of their more precious souls ? So they
argued, and God rewarded their confidence. He,
who never fails to keep faith with his servants,
stood by his Apostles and Martyrs before earthly
tribunals, and gave them strength to overcome in
the hour of their death, or, if he saw fit, provided
(sometimes miraculously) means for their escape.
And when his holy Confessors, hungering and thirst-
ing only after his love, despised the world and
neglected their own worldly interests, he provided
them with food and raiment and all their corporal
wants, and fed them besides, past all our imagining,
with the hidden sweetness of Divine Love.

THIRD POINT. *We must learn, then, to glorify
God in his Saints, who owed and attributed all their
sanctity to him.* God did not choose his Saints from
among those who had the greatest of worldly opportunities. Some of them—St. Francis for example
—had great opposition to overcome, and God over-
came it for them : some, like Blessed John Vianney,
were poor and ignorant, and God enlightened them
miraculously : some, like St. Mary Magdalen, were
sunk in the depths of sin, and he lifted them on to
their feet to serve him. What loving care, then,
does he bestow on those who earnestly seek for him !
They are strangers and pilgrims in this world of
shadows—it is he who refreshes their pilgrimage :
they are defenceless against their oppressors—it is
He who judges their cause ; they sacrifice, for His
sake, earthly loves and attachments—He more than
repays them with celestial delights. It is the
sinners who trust in worldly prosperity who find,
sooner or later, that even this world fails them.

The Lord shall reign for ever ; thy God, O Sion, unto generation and generation.

I will praise thee, O Lord, with my whole heart, for thou hast heard the words of my mouth.

I will sing praise to thee in the sight of the Angels : I will worship towards thy holy temple, and I will give glory to thy name ;

for thy mercy and for thy truth, for thou hast magnified thy holy name above all.

In what day soever I shall call upon thee, hear me.

Thou shalt multiply strength in my soul.

May all the kings of the earth give glory to thee,

Let us then adore God on his eternal throne, joining our praise with that of his heavenly Courtiers, while we implore their patronage.

Acts : Contempt of the world ; confidence in God's Providence ; congratulation with his Saints.

Colloquy with God who protects the weak and exalts the humble.

26. Ps. CXXXVII. (Confitebor tibi . . quoniam).

THE FAITHFUL DEPARTED.

FIRST POINT. *The souls in Purgatory are sure of their final salvation.* Whatever be the sufferings of Purgatory, the state of the faithful dead must yet be one that causes thankfulness, seeing that they have now been granted the prayer that is most solemn and urgent of all our prayers on earth—that for final perseverance. With the Angel Guardians that have brought them safely to the end of their pilgrimage, they can look forwards to the Heavenly City which is now their sure destination, and thank God for the certainty. Perhaps they see more clearly now that it was only his mercy, only his faithfulness, that saved them, for his own glory, from the pains of Hell. Though they can no longer merit, they can still pray, and feel (instead of blindly guessing, as they did on earth) the answer to their prayers. Weak and helpless so far as their own merits are concerned, they know now that, by God's gracious assistance, they will go on from strength to strength till they appear before him in Sion.

SECOND POINT. *They see earthly values in their true light.* The outward circumstances of life, which gave to one soul worldly superiority over

H

for they have heard all the words of thy mouth.

And let them sing in the ways of the Lord ;
for great is the glory of the Lord.

For the Lord is high, and looketh on the low,

and the high he knoweth afar off.

If I shall walk in the midst of tribulation,
thou wilt quicken me ; and thou hast stretched
forth thy hand against the wrath of my enemies,
and thy right hand hath saved me.

The Lord will repay for me :

thy mercy, O Lord, endureth for ever ; O
despise not the works of thy hands.

another, are now torn away ; riches, good birth, power, influence, personal attractiveness avail them nothing, and have lost their meaning : the stern lessons of Scripture on these subjects, often read and understood, but in many cases little meditated over and applied, now stand out evident to their view. They are all in one case, travelling together along the road by which God's Justice leads them to himself, and the thought of his glory now swamps and overshadows all lesser distinctions. Nay, in proportion as poverty, subjection, and misfortune, borne with patience and humility, won them favour with God, they find their lot in that world alleviated : in proportion as they were led to neglect God's claims and their neighbour's necessities through the pride of their prosperity, they have to suffer the temporal punishment due to them for their indifference.

THIRD POINT. *They suffer, and need our prayers.* They go forward, indeed, but by a way of purgation, in which the debts of their earthly life must be paid by suffering ; and we must join our prayers with theirs that God will refresh and revive their drooping spirits, and alleviate the pains which are now exacted from them by the sins that have become their tormentors. Not that they could ever pay the full debt ; it is our Lord himself who makes satisfaction, by the merits of his Passion, for the heinousness of their guilt. But his mercy does not stop there ; he hates nothing that he has made, and will remit something of that most merciful retribution in Purgatory, in answer to the prayers of the friends they have left on earth, till at last his creatures arrive at the destiny for which they were made —to know him and to enjoy him for all eternity.

My heart hath uttered a good word : I speak
my works to the King : my tongue is the pen
of a scrivener that writeth swiftly.

Thou art beautiful above the sons of men,
grace is poured abroad in thy lips :
therefore hath God blessed thee for ever.

Gird thy sword upon thy thigh, O thou most
mighty.

With thy comeliness and thy beauty set out :
proceed prosperously and reign.

Because of truth and meekness and justice :
and thy right hand shall conduct thee wonder-
fully.

Thy arrows are sharp : under thee shall the
people fall, into the hearts of the King's enemies.

Thy throne, O God, is for ever and ever ;
the sceptre of thy kingdom is a sceptre of
righteousness.

Thou hast loved justice and hated iniquity :
therefore God, thy God, hath anointed thee with
the oil of gladness above thy fellows.

Myrrh and stacte and cassia perfume thy
garments, from the ivory houses : out of which
the daughters of kings have delighted thee in
thy glory.

Acts : Prayer for perseverance ; contempt of the world's values; intercession for the faithful departed.

Colloquy with God who holds the issues of our life here and hereafter.

27. Ps. XLIV. (Eructavit cor meum).
THE PRAISES OF MARY.

FIRST POINT. *The glories of the Sacred Humanity.* There is no subject which can so readily excite our praise and admiration as the exaltation of our human Nature in Jesus Christ. In his whole life a beauty shines forth which is not of this world, although he is truly Man and circumscribed by the necessary limitations of humanity. His words are the words of eternal life, the unaging message of God's Revelation. Yet he comes to earth with a sword, for he divides the hearts of men according as they accept or reject his message. He is to reign as a King, full of love and of pardon, in the hearts of those who accept it; he enlightens them with his truth, inspires them with the example of his patience and humility, justifies them by His merits. But he is also a king in his condemnation of those who reject him, for his words are like sharp arrows, penetrating the conscience of his enemies, " that out of many hearts thoughts may be revealed. In this kingly capacity, justifying his servants and judging his enemies, the Son of Mary is to reign for ever, his manhood anointed beyond the possibilities of ordinary manhood by the unction which flows from its union with the Person of the Divine Word.

SECOND POINT. *The corresponding glories of the Mother of God.* The garment of the king—that is, the sacred Humanity assumed by the Son of God, derives its incorruptible fragrance—its freedom,

The queen stood on thy right hand
in gilded clothing,

surrounded with variety.

Hearken, O daughter, and see, and incline
thy ear ; and forget thy people and thy father's
house.

And the King shall greatly desire thy beauty ;
for he is the Lord thy God, and him shall they
adore.

And the daughter of Tyre with gifts, yea, all
the rich among the people, shall entreat thy
countenance.

All the glory of the King's daughter is within
in golden borders, clothed round about with
varieties.

After her shall virgins be brought to the king ;
her neighbours shall be brought to thee ;
they shall be brought with gladness and rejoicing ; they shall be brought into the temple of
the king.

Instead of thy fathers, sons are born to thee ;
thou shalt make them princes over all the earth.

that is, from the corruption we inherit from Adam
—from Mary, the Tower of Ivory, whose inexpugn-
able purity defied the assaults of sin. The first
place, therefore, in the King's court, must be given
to his Mother, who, like the gold that derives its
glory from the light which it reflects, won glory by
her perfect determination to correspond with God's
Will for her : from this single shining quality depend all the other graces we admire in her, her
purity, charity, unselfishness, humility, silence.
Sprung from the royal house of Juda, the women
of which were always proud of their motherhood,
hoping that the Messiah would one day be descended
from them, she forgets all this, silently making a
vow of virginity to God.   Therefore she is counted
worthy, in default of human wedlock, to have a
higher title as the Spouse of the Holy Ghost : she
achieves a higher dignity, and from that time forth
even the mightiest on earth bow down to entreat
her intercession.

THIRD POINT.   *Mary is the Queen of Virgins and
the Mother of the Church.*   Mary's perfect obedience
is an interior quality, hidden from human gaze by
her humble life and her love of silence, yet see the
manifold praises it claims from the Church ! This
correspondence with grace, combined with this
unselfish humility, must be shared to some extent
by all who would find a vocation in God's service ;
those who thus imitate her will be brought by her
patronage to the eternal felicity of the heavenly
Palace.   What are the royal names of David's line
compared with the spiritual succession of those
devout souls who, adorned by the imitation of her,
sustained by her prayers, mystically united with
her Son, have shewn forth the glory of God in all

They shall remember thy name throughout all generations, therefore shall the people praise thee, yea, for ever and ever.

We will praise thee, O God, we will praise,

and we will call upon thy name.

We will relate thy wondrous works.

When I shall take a time, I will judge justices.

The earth is melted, and all that dwell therein,

I have established the pillars thereof.

parts of the world, and by their willing tribute to the powerfulness of her prayers have helped to secure the fulfilment of the promise that all generations should call her blessed ?

Acts : Congratulation with Mary on the glories of her Son and the graces bestowed on her ; renunciation of all selfish ambition, as opposed to God's glory ; humility and desire of earthly obscurity.

Colloquy with Christ as the Spouse of the devout soul.

28. Ps. LXXIV. (Confitebimur tibi, Deus).
THE CHAIR OF PETER.

FIRST POINT. *The Mission of the Apostles to the world.* The Apostles will praise (literally " confess to ") God ; that is, they will attribute to Him all the glory he shews forth in them, not to themselves, as if he had made over to them his sovereignty : they will call upon His name, recognizing continually that he is their only source of strength, and "glorying in their infirmities." They will not use arguments of human wisdom ; they will simply "speak the things which they have seen and heard," leaving the Gospel to do its own work. And Saint Peter, when he has " taken a time " or opportunity (for God is never in a hurry, and develops his counsels by degrees), will begin to exercise publicly, with his successors, the judicial powers of binding and loosing conferred on him by Christ. The world as he finds it seems tottering to its fall : an unwieldy Empire, full of corruption, is (as its own poet confesses) " falling by its own weight " ; the ties of morality are sapped ; natural religion is melting away into a confused mass of false beliefs. To the

I said to the wicked : Do not act wickedly.
And to the sinners, Lift not up the horn.   Lift
not up your horn on high ; speak not iniquity
against God.

For neither from the East,
nor from the West,
nor from the desert hills :

· for God is the judge.
One he putteth down, and another he lifteth
up.

For in the hand of the Lord there is a cup of
strong wine full of mixture, and he hath poured
it out from this to that :

spiritual heirs of the Galilean fisherman it is given to hold up the twin pillars of Justice and Truth, and save the world's civilization from crumbling away.

SECOND POINT. *The spiritual Empire, through God's assistance, outlives the material force of the world's conquerors.* It is not to be supposed that the triumph of the Church will call forth no opposition from the world's rulers ; never is the Church so much herself as when she overpowers the evil-doer by the mere force of her spiritual predominance—Ambrose against Theodosius, Leo against Attila. The Church remains secure ; the secular powers God allows to arise in the world succeed one another like waves, and vanish as if they had not been, according to God's providential design. The Goths, Vandals, and Huns swarm in from the East ; their progress is finally checked by the rise of the Franks in the West ; the great Empire of the False Prophet spreads from the desert mountains of the South, and at last spends its force : whatever happens, happens at least through the permissive will of God, who puts down one and lifts up another, making Nero die as a fugitive, while the peasant he crucified sets up an empire which shall never be destroyed.

THIRD POINT. *God tempers prosperity and adversity in this world not according to human merits, reserving his judgments to the next.* Yet we cannot trace God's dealings in history as a simple triumph of spirit over brute force. The Church has her persecutions as well as her triumphs, her dry seasons as well as her times of growth, her unworthy as well as her worthy rulers. The chalice which God puts to the lips of his creatures is now sweet, now bitter, for the wormwood and the gall are necessary to our

But the dregs thereof are not emptied; all the sinners of the earth shall drink.

But I will declare for ever; I will sing to the God of Jacob.

And I will break all the horns of sinners, but the horns of the just shall be exalted.

How lovely are thy tabernacles, O Lord of Hosts !

My soul longeth and fainteth for the courts of the Lord ;

my heart and my flesh have rejoiced in the living God. For the sparrow hath found herself a house, and the turtle a nest for herself where she may lay her young ones,

thy altars, O Lord of Hosts, my King and my God.

spiritual progress, as well as the wine of his consolation.. But, when the last drop is drained and the time comes for judgment, we shall see that the bitterest dregs were reserved for eternity; that God, who ratifies in Heaven the decrees of His Church on earth, executes his full judgment against sinners in a future state. Meanwhile the Church continues to deliver the old message, sings the old hymns of praise, and experiences as ever the promise that the Gates of Hell shall not prevail against the Rock of Peter.

Acts : Loyalty to the Vicar of Christ ; thanksgiving for God's protection of his Church ; fear of judgment to come.

Colloquy with God who exalts the humble.

29. Ps. LXXXIII. (Quam dilecta).
THE CHOICE OF THE INTERIOR LIFE.

FIRST POINT. *The interior life our home.* As the Jewish Tabernacle was the *temporary* and *incomplete* foreshadowing of the Temple, so, in order to give us a foretaste of heaven, God has pitched his tent among us in our pilgrimage : the pursuit of the interior life ·does give a foretaste of the joys of heaven. Hence the spell which it casts over the souls of those God calls to it ; they cannot rest satisfied without it, cannot breathe freely in the stale air of the world. The interior consolation, as some of the Saints have noticed, even gives the sense of bodily well-being. The birds, to which God has given the glorious liberty of the air, yet return, year by year, to their chosen nests ; so the human soul, for all the free-will God has endowed it with, finds sooner or later that its need lies not in

Blessed are they that dwell in thy house, O Lord ; they shall praise thee for ever and ever.

Blessed is the man whose help is from thee.

In his heart he hath disposed to ascend by steps,

in the vale of tears, in the place which he hath set.

For the lawgiver shall give a blessing ;

they shall go from virtue to virtue :

The God of Gods shall be seen in Sion.

O Lord God of hosts, hear my prayer : give ear, O God of Jacob. Behold, O God our protector, and look on the face of thy Christ.

fresh adventures, but in a home : this home the interior soul finds in its intimate converse with God, in its self-oblation to him. Only in heaven is uninterrupted contemplation possible, but even on earth God gives some favoured souls the grace of long intercourse with him and almost continual recollectedness before him.

SECOND POINT. *But the interior life is also a journey.* Yet, when God gives us the initial graces and favours that attract us to the interior life, he is not calling us to a life of ease, but to a painful progress. Perseverance does not mean merely going on, it means going upward, and he who aspires to the interior life must make up his mind to the prospect of a gradual ascent, step by step—we cannot all at once breathe the mountain air, we must become accustomed to it by gradual stages of spiritual advance. Man, by his sin, has made the world a vale of tears, a place in which all spiritual development is contrary to nature, and so attainable only by mortification and painful struggle. But he who determines the hard conditions of our course himself sends us grace to persevere in spite of them : hopeless as the obstacles may seem at first, as they tower above us, we shall find that one step cut in the rock—one solid virtue acquired—will give us a foothold to begin the cutting of the next, and so on. However much or however little we approach in this world to perfect contemplation, this painful journey is at least a sure road to the open vision in Heaven.

THIRD POINT. *Holiness, even in a low degree, is worth the struggle.* Let us then ask humbly to be allowed to serve God in this way ; let us ask him to forget our weakness and worldliness, and to loo

For better is one day in thy courts above thousands.

I have chosen to be an abject in the house of my God, rather than to dwell in the tabernacles of sinners.

For God loveth mercy and truth :
the Lord will give grace and glory.
He will not deprive of good things them that walk in innocence. O Lord of hosts, blessed is the man that trusteth in thee.

To thee, O Lord, have I lifted up my soul.

In thee, O my God, I put my trust ; let me not be ashamed, neither let my enemies laugh at me,

for none of them that wait on thee shall be confounded.

Let all them be confounded that act unjust things without a cause.

upon our poor human nature as it is represented in Christ our Head. Even if we have, in his Providence, little more time left to us on earth, the feeble struggles of the beginner in holiness will avail us more than a long life spent in casual observance of our religion. Even if he does not mean to raise us to any great level of sanctity, the mere privilege of special attendance in his court, however menial be the office, is of more value than any position of worldly prominence in the midst of unchallenged imperfections. God is merciful, and does not despise the sinner ; faithful, and will not forget his promise ; he offers us sufficient grace for our needs, and glory hereafter, and he has spiritual blessings in store for us here if we persevere with a good intention, trusting only in his strength for our sanctification.

Acts : Desire for union with God, resolve of perseverance, humility in our spiritual aims.

Colloquy with God as our only source of rest and our only goal.

30. Ps. XXIV. (Ad te Domine levavi).
The Approach to the Interior Life.

First Point. *We must approach with the sense of unworthiness.* I lift up my soul—from what a depth !—to thee, my God—at what a height ! Only because of my confidence in thy grace can I master the sense of confusion which such an aspiration makes in me, my fear of the derision which I may think of it as causing to my spiritual enemies. Only because it is the soul's part to wait, thy part to act and to perform. It is only those who are all activity, working mischief to their own souls, who (if they knew it) should be confused. The humble

Shew, O Lord, thy ways to me,
and teach me thy paths.

Direct me in thy truth, and teach me, for
thou art God my Saviour, and on thee have I
waited all the day long.

Remember, O Lord, thy bowels of compassion,
and thy mercies that are from the beginning of
the world.

The sins of my youth, and my ignorances, do
not remember.

According to thy mercy remember thou me
for thy goodness' sake, O Lord.

The Lord is sweet and righteous; therefore
he will give a law to sinners in the way.

He will guide the mild in judgment; he will
teach the meek his ways.

All the ways of the Lord are mercy and truth,
to them that seek after his covenant and his
testimonies.

For thy name's sake, O Lord, thou wilt
pardon my sin, for it is great.

Who is the man that feareth the Lord? He
hath appointed him a law in the way he hath
chosen;
his soul shall dwell in good things, and his seed
shall inherit the land. The Lord is a firmament
to them that fear him, and his covenant shall
be made manifest to them.

My eyes are ever towards the Lord;

soul looks to God for all guidance in the choice of her common paths, or in the higher mountain-tracks of more perfect devotion ; takes God for her master and teacher in all the difficulties she may encounter ; content, herself, to wait upon God for her perfection—if need be, all her life long. I can appeal to no merits of my own in the past, only to God's mercies in my life, when I ask for fresh mercies in the future. My own influence on my life hitherto has been, too often, merely sin ; and where it was not sin, how often it has been blind and mis-directed effort ! Only in accordance with his mercy, only on the ground of his own self-diffusing goodness, can I ask God to regard me now.

SECOND POINT. *We must approach in a spirit of confidence.* How sweet, then, and how faithful are God's mercies, which he lavishes on us who are yet sinners, on us who are yet blindly struggling on our earthly pilgrimage. He asks only meekness and patience of us, in conforming ourselves to his will. No doubts, no temptations, no distractions that he permits can be anything but opportunities merci-fully sent to us, if we are faithfully seeking to obey him. No need to disguise my sinfulness ; his omnipotence takes delight in producing fruit from barren soil. To those who have the sincere inten-tion of living in the fear of God, he himself gives direction, sufficient for the vocation to which he has predestined them ; gives inward peace and happi-ness on earth, as well as the holy hope of immortal-ity ; gives support in all their temptations and trials by the faithful promise of his succour.

THIRD POINT. *We must approach with full consciousness of our own needs.* What can I do but turn my eyes patiently towards him, when I find my

for he shall pluck my feet out of the snare.

Look thou upon me, and have mercy on me, for I am alone and poor.

The troubles of my heart are multiplied; deliver me from my necessities, see my abjection and my labour, and forgive me all my sins.

Consider my enemies, for they are multiplied, and have hated me with an unjust hatred.

Keep thou my soul and deliver me ; I shall not be ashamed, for I have hoped in thee.

The innocent and the upright have adhered to me, because I have waited on thee.

Deliver Israel, O God, from all his tribulations.

I will extol thee, O Lord, for thou hast upheld me,

and hast not made my enemies to rejoice over me.

O Lord my God, I have cried to thee, and thou hast healed me.

feet entangled, past my own efforts to extricate them, in so much love of creatures, self-seeking, self-pride ? What can I ask but pity, seeing how helpless I am in myself, how poor of spiritual graces ? The more I try to live worthily of him, the more conscious I become of my many infirmities —so many humiliating defeats, so many struggles apparently unavailing ! Nor is it only myself I have to conquer : spiritual enemies, in blind hatred of all that is pleasing to God, seek to take advantage of my weakness : the more terrible my assailants show themselves, the more I am driven to my knees. And yet I am not destitute of allies ; for, if I wait patiently, the prayers of just men made perfect will petition for my release. Lord, when thy servant Jacob wrestled with thee in prayer, thou gavest him the name of Israel, because as a prince he had power with thee and with men : despise not then my prayers, but give me victory in thy good time.

Acts : Humility, confidence, sense of poverty.
Colloquy with God who alone can act in us.

31. Ps. XXIX. (Exaltabo te Domine, . . quoniam). .

EARLY DISCOURAGEMENTS.

FIRST POINT. *The soul looks back with inexpress-ible gratitude to her conversion, or preservation from sin.* As the conservation of our existence is due to a continual act of God's power, so our preservation from deadly sin is a continual act of his mercy : our spiritual enemies are all about us, like dogs waiting for their prey to be thrown to them. Most of us think little of the gift of health (which never-theless depends on the perfect functioning of so many minute organs) unless we have had experience

Thou hast brought forth, O Lord, my soul from heli ; thou hast saved me from them that go down into the pit.

Sing to the Lord, O ye his saints, and give praise to the memory of his holiness ; for wrath is in his indignation, and life in his good will.

In the evening weeping shall have place, and in the morning gladness.

And in my abundance I said, I shall never be moved :

O Lord, in thy favour thou gavest strength to my beauty.

Thou turnedst away thy face from me, and I became troubled.

To thee, O Lord, will I cry, and I will make supplication to my God.

of disease and recovery ; just so most of us, those especially who have never experienced the depths of sin and the relief of conversion, have grown accustomed to the ordinary grace of perseverance in the faith, and forget to give thanks as we ought. It is well for us, sometimes, to cast a terrified look over the edge of that abyss into which it is so easy to fall. Let us then give praise and thanks to God, the source of all holiness, whose indignation will be visited on those who provoke it with terrible retribution, of whose free gift it comes that our souls are alive to this day.

SECOND POINT. *Reflection on mercies in the past must not lead us to presume on future favours.* But we are not to suppose that, when we aspire higher towards a more perfect union with God, life will be all sunshine and peace. Day and night, we shall find, will alternate ; the darkness of desolation will be the necessary prelude to the fuller dawn of his presence. In spite of the abundant favours he showers upon us, especially when he is leading us on towards the interior life, we may not for one moment let our confidence rest upon the consciousness of them, even though it be accompanied by the humble recognition that we owe all to his gifts. We must be prepared at every moment for his hiding away his face, letting us fall into distractions, drynesses, perhaps even doubts and scruples. These will unavoidably lessen the direct sense of his presence which now enfolds us, but we are not to allow them to strike panic into the superior will, which must contrive to aspire faithfully towards him despite all discouragement.

THIRD POINT. *Though the soul may feel as if she experienced the pangs of spiritual death, she must*

What profit is there in my blood, whilst I go down to corruption ? Shall the dust confess to thee, or declare thy truth ?

The Lord hath heard, and hath had mercy on me ; the Lord became my helper.
Thou hast turned for me my mourning into joy,

thou hast cut my sackcloth, and hast compassed me with gladness. To the end that my glory may sing to thee, and I may not regret :
O Lord my God, I will give praise to thee for ever.

The Lord is my light

and my salvation ; whom shall I fear ?

still hope for release. Although such discourage-
ments are sent to us by God for our perfecting, it is
right to pray, so long as we do not pray impatiently,
that the chalice may be removed from us (as our
Saviour himself did). The spiritual faculties will be
so clouded and benumbed that we shall feel as if
our lives were useless to God, as if the prayers we
continue to offer with so little relish and conviction
must be unavailing and disregarded altogether. It
is not so ; God is only waiting for his own good time
to answer them and to give us the help of his
countenance once more. The desolations that lie
behind us will then add to our consolation ; the
garment of our humiliation will be changed into
hitherto inexperienced delight. We shall give
thanks then, without any sense of recrimination or
remonstrance with God, for the trials he has
suffered us to pass through, and our joy will be the
joy that no man takes from us.

Acts : Gratitude, resignation to all that God may
allow to befal our spiritual lives, hope and trust in
him.

Colloquy with God who made both light and darkness, and sees that they are good.

32. Ps. XXVI. (Dominus Illuminatio).

THE HIDDEN LIFE IS THE CHRISTIAN'S STRENGTH.

FIRST POINT. *Security of conscience arises from
trust in God.* The Lord is my *light* ; it is by his
illumination that I judge and am judged ; I need
not be afraid of any secret machinations while the
rays of this Sun make my path plain. He is my
salvation ; it is not any deeds of mine, but his

The Lord is the protector of my life ; of whom shall I be afraid ?

While the wicked draw near against me, to eat my flesh (*i.e.* calumniate me), my enemies have been weakened, and have fallen.

If armies in camp should stand together against me, my heart shall not fear.

If a battle should rise up against me, in this will I be confident.

One thing I have asked of the Lord, this will I seek after, that I may dwell in the house of the Lord all the days of my life,
that I may see the delight of the Lord,
and visit his temple.

For he hath hidden me in his tabernacle ; in the day of evils he hath protected me in the secret place of his tabernacle,

He hath exalted me upon a rock,

and now hath he lifted up my head above my enemies.

I have gone round, and have offered up in his tabernacle a sacrifice of jubilation ; I will sing and recite a psalm to the Lord.

Hear my voice, O Lord, with which I have cried to thee ; have mercy on me and hear me.

merciful Redemption that gives me leave to hope. He is the *protector* or *coverer* of my life ; his outstretched Hand shields me from the world's rebukes. Hence, when my fleshly enemies assail me with criticism, or the Devil (who by his very name is a False Accuser) tempts me to despair by the thought of my own sins, their efforts are unavailing. Even when it seems as if a *camp*, or fortified line, were drawn across my path of spiritual progress, I can confidently attack it ; and, if my enemies take the offensive, this fact (*i.e.* the fact that I am responsible to God only) will give me strength to resist.

SECOND POINT. *Therefore, in order to seek strength, I must develop the interior life.* Only one thing I ask of God, not that I may have no temptations, not that I may have no detractors, but that I may enjoy an interior intimacy with him ; that my appetite may be for the pleasures he only gives, and my refuge in trouble the sanctuary of his presence. The seclusion of interior prayer is a curtain or tent which at once makes me feel closer to him, and enables me to forget and disregard any attack from without ; just as a roof, however poor, gives a man comfort in a storm, while the very raging of the storm without makes him feel more intimate with his companions inside. Or I may think of prayer as a plateau of rock, on which a man escaping from his enemies is concealed, because the level of it is above their heads—so the interior life is unassailable, because it is beyond the reach of earthly minds. For this interior fastness I can never cease to *thank* and *praise* God, whose promises afford me such shelter.

THIRD POINT. *Diligence and patience needed for this intercourse with God.* As a man's face continually turns to look for something he is expecting, or

My heart hath said to thee, " My face hath sought thee,"
thy face, O Lord, will I still seek.

Turn not away thy face from me ; decline not in thy wrath from thy servant.

Be thou my helper, forsake me not ; do not thou despise me, O God my Saviour ;

For my father and my mother have left me, but the Lord hath taken me up.

Set me, O Lord, a law in thy way, and guide me in the right path because of mine enemies ; deliver me not over to the will of them that trouble me ; for unjust witnesses have risen up against me, and iniquity hath lied to itself.

I believe to see the good things of the Lord in the land of the living.

Expect the Lord : do manfully. And let thy heart take courage, and wait thou for the Lord.

Upon the rivers of Babylon, there we sat and wept, when we remembered Sion.

towards some special object of his affections, so the regard of the soul must continually be towards God —in attention, when his Face shines upon us, in aspiration, when he hides it, as he sometimes will. Only let us not deserve that through any fault of our own he should hide it *in displeasure*. He will not abandon us, unless he is first abandoned : we may lose the love of our closest friends without our fault, but not God's love. We must seek his face " as the eyes of servants wait on the hand of their masters " looking anxiously for any sign of what his will is for us ; we must be sure of his approbation if we are to avoid being filled with fears and scruples by consideration for human criticism. Further, we must believe that he is able to reward us, even in this life, with spiritual privileges : if they seem to be denied us, we must wait patiently, and fight on bravely in the dark, looking for his own good time in which he will turn and reward us.

Acts : Confidence, desire for God, patience to attend on his will.

Colloquy—ask for intimate communion with God, hidden from the world's distractions.

33. Ps. CXXXVI. (Super flumina).

THE SPIRIT OF DETACHMENT.

FIRST POINT. *The interior soul lives in the world as an exile.* Although our souls are, in the order of history, created first for earth and then for heaven, we are nevertheless in a sense exiles from a heavenly country, since we are immortal spirits imprisoned in time, and surrounded with the miserable conditions of fallen nature. As the river of time flows past us, our hearts are set, in painful longing, upon our true

On the willows in the midst thereof we hung up our instruments.

For they that led us into captivity required of us the words of songs, and they that carried us away said, " Sing ye to us a hymn of the songs of Sion."

How shall we sing the song of the Lord in a strange land ?

If I forget thee, O Jerusalem, let my right hand be forgotten : let my tongue cleave to my jaws, if I do not remember thee ;

If I make not Jerusalem the beginning of my joy.

home. We derive our inspiration, not from the scenes around us, but from a dimly imagined picture. And yet the world about us cannot understand this sadness ; cannot understand why we do not acclimatize ourselves to our surroundings, and throw ourselves heart and soul into its short-lived enjoyments ; cannot understand why our spirits are not keyed to the pitch of its frivolous melodies. Yet the reason is simple. In a fallen world, reminded at every turn of the misuse to which men put God's best gifts, the soul that has caught some echo of the heavenly music is forced to remain dumb and unresponsive.

SECOND POINT. *This homesickness must mean, not discontent with this world, but loyal affection for the next.* Christians are not meant to remain idle or voiceless in the world of our banishment : whatsoever our hand is able to do, we must do earnestly, and there is a time to speak as well as a time for silence. But it is better that our hands were cut off, or that our tongues should be for ever silenced, than that our absorption in human activities and human debates should make us forget for a moment the claims of the city we are destined to inherit. Hence arises a certain reservedness, among those who follow the interior life, about the use of natural enjoyments ; it is not that we are to cut ourselves off altogether from the beauties and the attractions of the world in which God has placed us, but that in all things we are bound, according to our ability, to prefer heaven to earth, the eternal to the transitory, by a conscious act of choice ; and that the root and principle of all our gladness, even in the most trivial circumstances, should be a pure intention to devote our lives in everything to the glory of God.

Remember, O Lord, the children of Edom in the day of Jerusalem, who say, Rase it, rase it, even to the foundation thereof.

O daughter of Babylon, miserable : blessed shall he be who shall repay thee thy payment which thou hast paid us.

Blessed shall he be that shall take and dash thy little ones against the rock.

Judge me, O God, and distinguish my cause from the nation that is not holy,

THIRD POINT. *Yet our conflict with nature and with the world will not be an easy victory.* Edom (or Esau) as opposed to Jacob symbolizes the natural as opposed to the spiritual man. The children of Edom, then, are those repugnances of corrupt nature which, until the time when God sees fit to free us more perfectly for his service, will continue to threaten with demolition the edifice which grace has so laboriously built up in our souls. And the daughter of Babylon—that is, the attractiveness of worldly honours and affections—will here be in alliance with nature ; we have to remind ourselves continually of the shortness and miseries of this life, that we may learn to despise it. Happy is he, in whom grace has proved the victor, and spoiled the spoiler of his prey ; happy is he, who has learned to throw down and break the world's temptations against the living Rock—a Stone of stumbling to many, and yet the chief Corner-stone of the celestial city ; the Rock which is Christ.

Acts: Detachment from the world, consecration to God of his own gifts, resolution to be on the watch against the seductions of nature.

Colloquy with Christ as the King of our true country claiming the loyalty of his exiled subjects.

34. Ps. XLII. (Judica me, Deus).
TEMPTATIONS TO WORLDLINESS.

FIRST POINT. *The world claims over us a false right of parentage, from which we must be emancipated.* We have recourse to God as our Judge and our Patron, appealing to him to give sentence against the claim of the world, which would make of us its children and its citizens, whereas we know

K

deliver me from the unjust and deceitful man.

For thou art God my strength : why hast thou cast me off ?

And why do I go sorrowful whilst the enemy afflicteth me ?

Send forth thy light and thy truth ;

They have conducted me, and brought me unto thy holy hill,

and into thy tabernacles.

And I will go in to the altar of God,

that by baptism we have become children of grace and members of a royal nation. Yet the world is full of plausible excuses, constantly appealing to our corrupt nature as if that were our true self. At times this claim is so insistent that we feel as if God had cut us off from our inheritance, although he himself is the very witness on whom we rely. How can this be ? It may be as a punishment for some infidelity to grace, for which we should implore his pardon : it may be only to test our loyalty : in either case, with whatever heaviness of heart, we must go forward (*incedo*), never yielding an inch to the importunacy of our adversary.

SECOND POINT. *To this end, we must pray to be allowed to see the world and our souls in a divine light.* Let us then earnestly contemplate the *truths* our holy Religion reveals to us : our fallen state, the price paid for our ransom, the destiny, heaven or hell, that lies before us. Let us ask for *light* to see ourselves as we are—creatures made out of nothing, helpless in our own strength, half-hearted in our desire for perfection : to see God as he is, infinitely holy, possessing all rights over us as our Creator and our Father. Thus we shall be brought to the foot of his holy hill—the mountain of perfection, up the slopes of which we must strive painfully, though it be a Calvary : God's truth will still keep our faces set forward, his light still illuminate our path. But we shall also be brought to his tabernacles, his meeting-place with men on their pilgrimage—to a growing intimacy with him, as the truth makes us more sure of his presence, and the light shews us something of its beauty.

THIRD POINT. *Meanwhile we have no reason to be discouraged, so long as we offer ourselves generously.*

to God who giveth joy to my youth.

To thee, O God, my God, I will give praise
upon the harp : why art thou sad, O my soul ?
And why dost thou disquiet me ?

Hope in God, for I will still give praise to him,

the salvation of my countenance, and my God.

How good is God to Israel, to them that are
of a right heart !

But my feet were almost moved, my steps
had wellnigh slipped ;

because I had a zeal on occasion of the wicked,
seeing the prosperity of sinners.

For there is no regard to their death,
nor is there strength in their stripes.

In the outer court of the tabernacle stood the altar for whole burnt-offerings. And we, if we are to enter his tabernacles, must first offer ourselves to him without reserve. It is from him that we derive our existence itself, and all the happiness we enjoy ; it is but his right that we should offer it back to him. So, whether in heaviness or in gladness, every mood of ours will be turned into a melody in his honour : we will not allow the persistence of temptations to distract or disquiet us in his service. There could be no Christian virtue of hope, if God did not test even his chosen with darkness and difficulties. Thanks to his infinite mercies, I need never blush to appear before Him, who, however weak my efforts and however low my state of prayer, is not ashamed to be called *my* God.

Acts: Protestation of fidelity to God's service : unconditional offering of self : resolve of perseverance.

Colloquy with God as the Patron who vindicates us to himself.

35. Ps. LXXII. (Quam bonus).
THE PROSPERITY OF THE WORLDLY.

FIRST POINT. *Apparent prosperity of the worldly.* We know that God cares especially for his own servants, and rewards, even in this world, their pure intentions. And yet, as we climb the painful hillpath towards the mountain of perfection, now and again our foot seems to slip when we look back at what we have left behind. We see those who are neither reconciled with God nor just to their fellowmen apparently undisturbed in their peace of conscience. The thought of death does not appal them : when trouble comes they derive, we know not whence, a sort of Stoical courage. When times

They are not in the labour of men, neither
shall they be scourged like other men. Therefore pride hath held them fast ; they are covered
with their iniquity and their wickedness.

Their iniquity hath come forth, as it were
from fatness ; they have passed into the affection of the heart.

They have thought and spoken wickedness,
they have spoken iniquity on high ; they have
set their mouth against heaven, and their tongue
hath passed through the earth.

Therefore will my people return here, and
full days shall be found in them : and they said,
How doth God know ?   And is there knowledge
in the most High ?   Behold, these are sinners ;
and yet abounding in the world they have
obtained riches.

And I said, Then have I in vain justified my
heart, and washed my hands among the innocent,
and I have been scourged all the day, and my
chastisement hath been in the mornings.

If I said, I will speak thus, behold, I should
condemn the generation of thy children.

I studied that I might know this thing ; it
is a labour in my sight, until I go unto the
sanctuary of God ;

And understand concerning their last ends.

But indeed for deceits thou hast put it to
them ; when they were lifted up thou hast
cast them down.

How are they brought to desolation !   They
have suddenly ceased to be ; they have perished
by reason of their iniquity.

are bad all round, these are often the people least affected by it. And the effect of this on their souls is to give them a good conceit of themselves, so that they never seem to feel the need of heavenly aid. They feel so secure that they will sometimes even glory in their worldliness, and the ease with which they gain the objects of their desire ; they talk arrogantly and blasphemously, as if they had scaled heaven and made conquest of earth. Small wonder that the simple servants of God should be distracted by their example, and given scandal by their prosperity, beginning to wonder if, after all, there is a God in Heaven, or a God who marks and cares for human fortunes, if sinners can so thrive on their ill-gotten gains with impunity.

SECOND POINT. *The devout soul will be fortified against worldly judgments.* And we, who have transferred the centre of our hopes to the next world, do not we too sometimes hesitate, as if all our careful custody of the senses, our mortifications, our constant spiritual exercises, might after all have been undertaken in vain ? Yet we have only to frame such a thought in order to see that it is impossible ; are we to brush aside the history and the testimony of all God's Saints ? We shall not solve the riddle in an arm-chair, but only on our knees, only when, enlightened by prayer, we view this human prosperity in the light of death and eternity. Then we see that there is no injustice which will not claim its punishment, no pride that will not be visited by humiliation. A sudden accident, and the unjust soul is hurled into eternity, to answer without delay for its crimes ; meantime, the world rolls on, and forgets its proud conquerors before the grass has sprung up over their graves.

As the dream of them that awake, O Lord, so in thy city thou shalt bring their image to nothing.

For my heart hath been inflamed, and my reins have been changed :

And I am brought to nothing,

And I knew not.

I am become as a beast before thee,

And I am always with thee ; thou hast held me by my right hand, and by thy will hast thou conducted me, and with thy glory thou hast received me.

For what have I in heaven ? And besides thee what do I desire upon earth ? For thee my flesh and my heart hath fainted away : thou art the God of my heart and my portion for ever.

For behold, all they that go far from thee shall perish ; thou hast destroyed all them that are disloyal to thee.

But it is good for me to adhere to my God, to put my hope in the Lord God, that I may declare all thy praises in the gates of the daughter of Sion.

Judge me, O Lord, for I have walked in my innocence,

THIRD POINT. *The gradual annihilation of self must quell these unruly motions in us.* Such indignation as we have been considering, though righteous in its motive, is unbecoming to an interior soul, which should avoid all inordinate motions of anger. By God's grace, if we keep still and let him work in us, we shall be brought to feel what we really are—that is, nothing; we shall learn the limitations of our knowledge—that is, that we know nothing. Our souls will be dumb and passive under God's exercising, like patient beasts that do not reason or remonstrate, but wait for the reins or the whip. When we have become thus passive and responsive, we shall know that God is near to direct us, that he holds us by the hand, leads us by interior motions along the way he has chosen, fits us for future glory. There will be, for us, only one end and object in heaven or earth —God himself; we shall fear nothing except absence from him, he will be our only hope, enjoyment, and reward. To be for one moment and in the least degree disobedient to him will be an infidelity crying out for punishment in hell; the sole good and meaning of life will be closer and ever closer union with him, fitting us for an eternity spent in proclaiming his praise.

Acts: Resolution against inordinate anger: self-annihilation.

Colloquy in which we compare ourselves to dumb beasts.

36. Ps. XXV. (Judica me Domine, quoniam).
DESIRE FOR PURITY OF INTENTION.

FIRST POINT. *True devotion involves the purifying of our inward thoughts.* As God will judge us

and I have put my trust in the Lord, and shall not be weakened.

Prove me, O Lord, and try me ;

burn my reins and my heart.

For thy mercy is before my eyes, and I am well pleased with thy truth : I have not sat with the council of vanity, neither will I go in with the doers of unjust things. I have hated the assembly of the malignant, and with the wicked I will not sit.

I will wash my hands among the innocent,

and will encompass thy altar, O Lord.

That I may hear the voice of thy praise, and tell of all thy wondrous works.

after death, so from moment to moment he reads infallibly the secrets of our hearts ; and we set ourselves too low a standard of innocence if we do not aspire to a purity of intention which can satisfy that piercing scrutiny. This path on which we desire to set our feet is a very narrow one ; only through his grace can we hope for strength to stumble in it less often. And the strength will not be won easily, but only through temptations which will prove us and perfect us. The purifying of our hearts, in this world as in the world to come, can only be " so as by fire " ; so much unsuspected dross is there, even in our purest ambitions, which needs to be burned away. Our thoughts continually tend to rest in vain and transitory consolations— we must not let them rest there : tend to lose themselves in uncharitable or self-satisfied criticisms of our neighbour—we must forbid them access to such subjects : tend even, at times, to remonstrate with God when his treatment of us seems, to our limited vision, harsh and neglectful—we must shrink from the bare idea of such impiety.

SECOND POINT. *This purification is not an end in itself, but a condition enabling us to offer ourselves to God.* We must beware of putting this aim of " self-improvement " before us as the end of our spiritual life ; it is not so. As we make our confessions in order to put ourselves in a right disposition for the receiving of the Most Holy Sacrament, so we should desire to purify our hearts only as a preliminary to offering them, an acceptable sacrifice, to God. The laver stands in the outer court of the tabernacle only to give access to the altar of holocausts. The true end of the spiritual life is to enable man to take his part in the sacrifice of praise

I have loved, O Lord, the beauty of thy house, and the place where thy glory dwelleth.

Take not away my soul, O God, with the wicked, nor my life with bloody men ; in whose hands are iniquities, their right hand is filled with gifts.

But as for me, I have walked in my innocence ; redeem me, and have mercy on me.

My foot hath stood in the direct way ; in the churches I will bless thee, O Lord.

which goes up to God continually from all his creatures. It passes, then, to the altar of holocausts and thence on to the Tabernacle itself, whose ornaments are of gold instead of brass, the Tabernacle of pure contemplation, where the glory of God is present to man (according to his measure) even in the state of pilgrimage.

THIRD POINT. *Whatever point of innocence we attain, we must remember that at every moment it is only grace that saves us from deadly sin.* However high we may advance (or think ourselves to have advanced) in the spiritual life, our prayer must continually be for the grace which still preserves us from the most heinous sins. But for this grace, we might be on the road to damnation with the impious, who turn their backs upon God, with brawlers and murderers, with those who shut their ears to the cry of justice and thrive on ill-gotten gains. Never dare we give thanks for our comparatively blameless conversation, without renewing our prayer to be saved from ourselves and forgiven for the sinful motions which, but for grace, might have plunged our souls into far worse misery than we have ever known. Thanks be to God, that in spite of our faltering steps and our continual falls, at least our faces are set in the right direction, and we can claim for ourselves the company of God's faithful servants, on earth and in heaven alike, as our fellow travellers towards our eternal goal.

Acts : Desire for purity of intention, dedication of all our best efforts to God ; fear and humility as we think what we might have been.

Colloquy with our Judge, who reads our most secret thoughts.

I have loved, because the Lord will hear the voice of my prayer, because he hath inclined his ear unto me ; and in my days I will call upon him.

The sorrows of death have compassed me, and the perils of hell have found me.

I met with trouble and sorrow,

and I called upon the name of the Lord, O Lord, deliver my soul.

The Lord is merciful and just, and our God sheweth mercy : the Lord is the Keeper of little ones. I was humbled, and he delivered me.

Turn, O my soul, into thy rest,

for the Lord hath been bountiful to thee ;

for he hath delivered my soul from death,

my eyes from tears, my feet from falling.

I will please the Lord in the land of the living.

I have believed, therefore have I spoken, but I have been humbled exceedingly ; I said in my excess, Every man is a liar.

What shall I render to the Lord for all the things that he hath rendered to me ?

37. Pss. CXIV, CXV, (Dilexi and Credidi, which form one Psalm in the Hebrew).

EASTER :—MORTIFICATION OUR DEBT TO THE
RISEN CHRIST.

FIRST POINT. *Christ has conquered death for us.*
In my days—that is, in the days of this earthly life,
which seems so short and uncertain, I can still turn
lovingly to God and claim his attention. The
circumstances of mortality all around may well
terrify me, still more the thought of what lies after
death ; the many miseries of our present position
teach the same lesson. Yet the Christian knows
that in life or death his soul is in the hands of a
faithful and merciful Creator ; humbly, because
we know our own helplessness, we turn to him for
our final deliverance. Cease, my soul, to fret and
to be alarmed over the troubles of this life ; repose
joyfully upon God's promise ; for in his mercy
(made known to us by his Resurrection) he takes
away the sting of death by the assurance of im-
mortality, the pang of sorrow by the thought of
future rewards, the tyranny of sin by the grace he
won for us in the Passion. In this earthly life, then,
which is the only space given to us for our probation, let us strive to please God who alone is the
source of all life.

SECOND POINT. *In return, he asks for our
mortification.* It is only our faith in the risen
Christ which makes it possible for us to explain life
as we find it ; if we look to any human comfort or
support, how illusory it all is—how even the best of
friends may fail us ! Christ has *given back* to us our
whole interest in life, what then do we owe him in
return ? He asks us to accept the Cup of Salvation

I will take the chalice of salvation,

and I will call upon the name of the Lord.

I will pay my vows to the Lord before all his people.

Precious in the sight of the Lord is the death of his saints.

O Lord, for I am thy servant ;

I am thy servant,
and the son of thy handmaid,

thou hast broken my bonds.

I will sacrifice to thee the sacrifice of praise, and I will call upon the name of the Lord.

I will pay my vows to the Lord in the sight of áll his people, in the courts of the house of the Lord, in the midst of thee, O Jerusalem.

he holds to our lips. But the Cup of Salvation is also the Cup of suffering—the Cup he drained in Gethsemane, and invited his Apostles, James and John, to share with him. This cup I will take, calling upon him to help me in enduring it, and giving thanks for the honour he thus does me : for the God whose chief friends and courtiers are the Martyrs and Confessors clearly attaches a special value to the endurance of suffering, such as he may demand of me.

THIRD POINT. *This claim, which he makes on our gratitude, he might have made on our obedience.* Man's soul is the slave of God ; his slave, because made by him out of nothing, and therefore destitute of all personal rights as against him ; his slave, because a member of Eve's family, and having both inherited and repeated the sin of his first parents, thus outlawing himself from grace ; his slave, because bought back from the captivity of sin by the ransom of the Precious Blood. Then let me make my whole life a holocaust of praise to God : in my life and in my death, in my trials and in my blessings, may his holy name be praised everywhere. Let me pay my vows, that is, acknowledge myself eternally his debtor, in the sight of all his saints and Angels this day.

Acts : Faith in the fact and the power of the Resurrection ; gratitude for it ; offering to God of present and future mortifications.

Colloquy with Christ who has broken our bonds

Why have the Gentiles raged, and the people devised vain things ? The Kings of the earth stood up, and the princes met together, against the Lord and against his Christ.

Let us break their bonds asunder, and let us cast away their yoke from us.

He that dwelleth in heaven shall laugh at them, and the Lord shall deride them.

Then shall he speak to them in his anger, and trouble them in his rage.

But I am appointed King by him
over Sion his holy mountain,

preaching his commandment.

38. Ps. II. (Quare fremuerunt).
THE TRIUMPH OF THE CROSS.

FIRST POINT. *Christ calls upon you to resist the tyranny of his enemies.* The crowd is making a dull, confused noise round Calvary : behind the crowd is a small and malignant conspiracy of the great ones of the earth. The murmur of the crowd is the roaring of the world about your ears, deafening you to heavenly sounds, while the evil spirits or those bad companions or temptations which have so much power in this world conspire to enslave you.

" Let us break their bonds " etc. : see the condescension with which Christ invites you to share in the work of emancipating your soul. We must shake off *their* yoke, and take up Christ's, carry the cross ; we must break *their* chains, and allow ourselves to be bound to a cross by the chains of love. In spite of their noise and their numbers, God can very easily give us the victory if we accept this invitation ; nay, he will visit with terrible punishment the tempters and those who suffer themselves to fall into temptation.

SECOND POINT. *Christ on the Cross is the revelation of the Divine Nature.* Christ reigns from the Cross, Jerusalem rises over the plain, Calvary over Jerusalem, the Cross over Calvary. The Crucifixion takes place on God's favourite, chosen mountain—he came to his own, and his own received him not. " Preaching his commandment "—what commandment ? " This is my precept, that ye love one another " ; this second Sermon on the Mount preaches the law of LOVE, wherein God manifests his own Nature to us.

The Lord hath said to me, " Thou art my Son ; this day have I begotten thee ;

ask of me,

and I will give thee the Gentiles for thy inheritance, and the utmost parts of the earth for thy possession ; thou shalt rule them with a rod of iron, and shalt break them in pieces like a potter's vessel."

And now, O ye Kings, understand : receive instruction, you that judge the earth.

Serve the Lord with fear, and rejoice unto him with trembling.

Embrace discipline lest at any time the Lord be angry, and you perish from the just way.

When his wrath shall be kindled in a short time, blessed are all they that trust in him.

A hymn, O God, becometh thee in Sion,

" Thou art my Son ; this day have I begotten thee " ; " to-day " because the generation of the Son is outside time ; the phrase " thou art my Son " is used when Christ is manifested as specially pleasing the Father—at his Baptism, his Transfiguration, surely also at his Crucifixion—" Begotten thee " in a special sense ; Christ suffers as the Head of Creation.

THIRD POINT. *Christ on the Cross draws all men to him.* " Ask of me "—the Father is still speaking ; by the Sacrifice of the Cross Christ is able to claim our redemption ; his desire is that he may reign in the hearts of all men. He wants to break our hearts with true contrition, to rule and guide them with the iron rod of mortification. Each of us has his soul for a kingdom, we can only govern it by understanding the lesson just given us. From the reference to God's wrath we must learn to fear his punishments ; from the sufferings of the Crucified we must learn to mortify ourselves. There is an end even of God's patience with sinners : what if we should set our feet on the wrong road, the road to Hell ? God's judgments in time are sometimes very sudden, and when they happen, blessed are all they that trust in him—let us learn betimes to put our trust in him who alone can save us in the hour of such visitations.

Acts : Desire of mortification, desire for final perseverance, fear, confidence in God.

Colloquy with Christ throned on Calvary.

39. Ps. LXIV. (Te decet hymnus).
DISPOSITIONS FOR DEVOUT COMMUNION.

FIRST POINT. *Direction of intention.* This, like every act of devotion we pay to God, is no more

and a vow shall be paid to thee in Jerusalem.

O hear my prayer; all flesh shall come to thee.

The words of the wicked have prevailed over us ;
and thou wilt pardon our transgressions.

Blessed is he whom thou hast chosen and taken to thee ; he shall dwell in thy courts.

We shall be filled with the good things of thy house ; holy is thy temple, wonderful in justice.

Hear us, O God our Saviour,

who art the hope of all the ends of the earth, and in the sea afar off.

Thou who preparest the mountains by thy strength, being girded with power, who troublest the depth of the sea, the noise of its waves.

The Gentiles shall be troubled, and they that

than we owe to him as his creatures, in mere recognition of his glory. We owe it to him again as his debtors, in gratitude for all our temporal and spiritual blessings. Yet he allows us, over and above this, to offer it to him for our own intentions ; and the principal intention of all must be that his holy will may be done and his holy Name magnified by all creatures. We must offer it also for the pardon of the sins we have committed through listening to the voice of temptation ; we must offer it in reparation for all the dishonour done to him by sinful and unworthy communions. We must offer it in petition for grace, that we may be worthy of his special vocation for us, that we may be still more closely and inseparably united to him, that we may receive to the fullest possible extent the fruits of this Sacrament, and draw fresh sanctification, as we draw our justification, from the Body broken and the Blood shed for us.

SECOND POINT. *Acts of faith, hope, and adoration.* We must believe in Christ, who thus gave his own Body on the Cross as the medicine which should restore us our spiritual health, and gives it to us now as the food by which that health is to be maintained and strengthened. We must hope in him, because there is no other Name under heaven whereby we may be saved, nor any tempestuous sea of doubts, difficulties, or misfortunes in which, though he seem to be asleep and inattentive to our prayers, we are not to look to him for deliverance. We must adore him, though he be now hidden from our sight by sacramental veils, as the God who created all things from the beginning, and still operates in every operation of nature around us ; who reveals himself, even to the natural reason, at

dwell in the uttermost borders shall be afraid at thy signs; thou shalt make the outgoings of the morning and of the evening to be joyful.

Thou hast visited the earth, and hast plentifully watered it;

thou hast many ways enriched it.

The river of God is filled with water; thou hast prepared their food, for so is its preparation.

Fill up plentifully the streams thereof, multiply its fruits,

it shall spring up and rejoice in its showers.

Thou shalt bless the crown of the year of thy goodness;
and thy fields shall be filled with plenty.

The beautiful places of the wilderness shall grow fat,
and the hills shall be girded about with joy.

The rams of the flock are clothed,
and the vales shall abound with corn,
they shall shout, yea, they shall sing a hymn.

Hear, O God, my prayer, and despise not my supplication; be attentive to me and hear me.

once in the terrors of the lightning, the wind and
the storm, and at the same time in the pale flush
of dawn and the mellow glories of the sunset.

THIRD POINT. *Acts of love and desire.* He is so
eager to claim our love, that it is not enough for
him to have come once to earth to tread the wine-
press of salvation ; he comes again and again to
inebriate us with its fruits. The grace once gained
he offers to increase without limit in answer to our
prayers. What but the torrents of divine mercy
could have produced such an endless store of
spiritual refreshment, to strengthen us on our way
to the full fruition of God ? May this heavenly
Wine ever inebriate us with fresh fervour, this
heavenly Wheat ever bring forth in us a fresh
harvest of good living ; and meanwhile, may he
grant us some drops of sensible devotion to sweeten
our spiritual growth. May he crown the work of
grace in us at every point ; sanctifying for us the
dull level of our daily occupations, the difficult
mortification of drynesses in prayer, the heights of
prayer at which we seem closest to him, the pasture-
land of our spiritual reading, the valleys of humiliation and self-distrust, that every mood of our
interior life may be, as we mean this communion to
be, a pure act of praise to his Name.

Acts : As above.

Colloquy with Jesus in the Blessed Sacrament

40. Ps. LIV. (Exaudi Deus orationem).
THE CLOISTER.

FIRST POINT. *The privilege of escaping from the
world.* God will not despise the lowliness of my
prayer now that he has allowed me to take the
lowest place among those specially dedicated to

I am grieved in my exercise,

and am troubled at the voice of the enemy, and at the tribulation of the sinner.

For they have cast iniquities upon me, and in wrath they were troublesome to me; my heart is troubled within me,

and the fear of death is fallen upon me.

Fear and trembling are come upon me,

and darkness hath covered me.

And I said, Who will give me wings like a dove, and I will fly and be at rest.

Lo, I have gone far off flying away, and I abode in the wilderness.

I waited for him that hath saved me from pusillanimity of spirit, and a storm.

Cast down, O Lord, and divide their tongues, for I have seen iniquity and contradiction in the city.

Day and night shall iniquity surround it upon its walls,

and in the midst thereof are labour and injustice,

and usury and deceit have not departed from its streets.

him. When I was in the world, my spiritual exercises seemed to bring me no peace, but rather to put me out of harmony with my surroundings ; the voice of temptation sounded terribly close in my ear all the while, and the thoughtless lives of others gave me a low standard of progress ; self-seeking and uncharitableness seemed to flourish around me, and weighed upon my spirits. For my weakness, my heart began to fail me ; how easy it would be for one so frail and so fickle to lose eternal life ! Doubts and scruples began to assail me ; darkness came upon my spirit, and blotted out for me the sun of worldly happiness, till nothing seemed to have any attraction or savour for me. I longed, then, for a vocation to the religious life, that would set my soul free to take its flight in undisturbed prayer, and would give rest to my troubled conscience. By God's mercy, I was enabled to carry out this flight, and, withdrawing into myself, to live *solus cum solo*, alone with the unapproachable God. It has been my part to wait patiently till God should see fit to strengthen my feeble courage and let me cheerfully breast the storm.

SECOND POINT. *Yet temptations are the heritage of my nature, and I must expect to find them in the cloister too.* May God still be with me to confound the devices of my spiritual enemies. For, although I have secured myself from without, making fast, as it were, the drawbridges of my spiritual citadel, I know that there is still treachery and disaffection within the camp : night and day I have still to be on my guard against my own infidelities. The arduousness of spiritual labours still daunts me, self-love still bears its sway : and where I thought that I had made the way clear for God, unsuspected

For if my enemy had reviled me, I would verily have borne with it, and if he that hated me had spoken great things against me, I would perhaps have hid myself from him.

But thou, a man of one mind, my guide and my familiar, who didst take sweet meats together with me ;

in the house of God we walked with consent.

Let death come upon them, and let them go down alive into hell, for there is wickedness in their dwellings, in the midst of them.

But I have cried to God, and the Lord will save me.

.Evening and morning and at noon I will speak and declare, and he shall hear my voice. He shall redeem my soul in peace from them that draw near to me, for among many they were with me.

God shall hear, and the Eternal shall humble them.

For there is no change with them, and they have not feared God ; he hath stretched forth his hand to repay : they have defiled his covenant, they are divided by the wrath of his countenance, and his heart hath drawn near ; his words are smoother than oil, and the same are darts.

relics of self-seeking and impure motives yet remain to be cast out. Alas, it was comparatively easy for me to resist the temptations that came clearly from without, disguised under no false colours ; the world boastfully claimed me as its prey, but its very boastfulness put me on my guard and warned me to hide myself in prayer. But now it is my own human spirit that is the source of my imperfections, the temperament that was born with me and has grown up with me from childhood ; the bad habits that I have even encouraged in myself, not realising that they were such, that survived undetected my earlier examinations of conscience. O may God send me grace to mortify these, and bury them in my Saviour's tomb ; I see now how hideous they are in his sight.

THIRD POINT. *But we must not be alarmed ; God will perfect his work in us.* Yet surely, if I am patient, God will not suffer his own work to perish ; if I remain faithful to my rule of prayer and the duties of my state, he will find fresh ways of escape. He will subdue in me these multitudinous roots of evil that seem so closely entwined around my very being ; the Eternal God keeps an unhurrying pace, but he will aid me at last. They are defrauding him of his honour, defying his sovereignty—he will be jealous for his own glory : they mar the performance of my bounden homage to him—he will claim his own rights, and his Sacred Heart will come to demand my love ; his words, full óf gentleness and of healing, will yet pierce me like a sword while I have imperfections to overcome. Let me only learn to wait patiently, casting all my scruples and anxieties before him.; he will teach me to progress steadily and unwaveringly towards him,

Cast thy care upon the Lord, and he shall sustain thee ; he shall not suffer the just to waver for ever. But thou, O Lord, shalt bring them down into the pit of destruction : bloody and deceitful men shall not live one half their days, but I will trust in thee, O Lord.

O Lord, remember David, and all his meekness ;

how he swore to the Lord, and vowed a vow to the God of Jacob : If I shall enter into the tabernacle of my house, if I shall go up into the bed wherein I lie, if I shall give sleep to my eyes or slumber to my eyelids or rest to my temples, until I find out a place for the Lord, a tabernacle for the God of Jacob.

Behold, we have heard of it in Ephrata ; we have found it in the fields of the wood.

We will go into his tabernacle ; we will adore in the place where his feet stood.

rooting out all in me that offends him before he calls me from my earthly labours to a heavenly reward.

Acts : Gratitude, resolve of watchfulness, patient confidence.

Colloquy with God as our hiding-place against the storms of temptation.

41. Ps. CXXXI. (Memento Domine).

MAINTENANCE OF THE SPIRIT OF AN INSTITUTE.

FIRST POINT. *Where we are slack about the obligations of our state, the memory of our human founder should fill us with confusion.* We appeal to God to hear our prayers through the cherished memory of our founder ; let us remind ourselves, in doing so, how far we have fallen short of our model. Our institute was founded in great meekness of obedience and of mutual forbearance ; how often have we given scandal by self-will and self-seeking ! It was founded in heroic labours, which admitted of no rest in body or mind, and involved sleepless nights of anxiety or of prayer ; how poor is our record of watchfulness, of industry, of mortification, when judged by that human standard ! It was a work of such toil to found our institute, to enshrine in human observance the cult of this particular mystery or grace ; are we to neglect the easier task of perpetuating it ? The plan was first conceived, the life was first started, in rough, primitive surroundings, a Subiaco or a Manresa, and from small beginnings ; every chance, then, seemed to be against it : now it has expressed itself solidly in elaborate buildings, smoothly-running organization, crowded churches etc. : shall we not, thus privileged, follow lovingly in the footsteps already marked out for us ?

Arise, O Lord, into thy resting place, thou, and the ark which thou hast sanctified.

Let thy priests be clothed with justice, and let thy saints rejoice ; for thy servant David's sake turn not away the face of thy Anointed.

The Lord hath sworn truth to David, and he will not make it void ; of the fruit of thy womb will I set upon thy throne.

If thy children will keep my covenant, and these my testimonies which I shall teach them, their children also for evermore shall sit upon thy throne.

For the Lord hath chosen Sion, he hath chosen it for his dwelling.

This is my rest for ever and ever ; here will I dwell, for I have chosen it.

Blessing I will bless her widow ;

I will satisfy her poor with bread ;

I will clothe her priests with salvation, and her saints shall rejoice with exceeding great joy.

There will I bring forth a horn to David ; I have prepared a lamp for my Anointed.

SECOND POINT. *Yet our trust must be in God, not in ourselves.* It was for God that this Institute was founded, that his Name might rest here, honoured and adored by us ; that he might dwell among us as in his temple through our common sanctification. Let us then, pleading on our own behalf the prayers of our founder, whether on earth or in heaven, implore all the graces our Saviour won for us by his Passion ; that our directors and all those in authority over us may be guided rightly, and their subjects be filled with the joy of the Holy Spirit. We need not be afraid ; by the mere fact that he raised up our first founders, God has shewn it to be his will that our work should continue and flourish through the centuries ; so long at least as we are honestly resolved to remain true to our spirit, and to correspond readily with every indication God gives of his purpose for us. And though we confess ourselves inferior to our fathers in our degree of holiness, for their sakes he will not allow their successors to die out.

THIRD POINT. *It is for God's sake, not for ours, that the Institute exists.* God, although he does not dwell in temples made with hands, does nevertheless single out certain places and certain institutions for the manifesting of his glory. Here, then, by his special favour, he dwells for ever ; we are only his tenants for the brief lease of our lives. We renounce earthly ties and pleasures that we may be wedded to him ; we renounce earthly goods that all our sufficiency may be of him ; our priests minister to us only as his stewards ; our happiness must all come from him and be devoted to him. We are here to reflect our founder's spirit ; and what was that but a tiny lamp kindled from the furnace of

M

His enemies I will clothe with confusion, but upon him shall my sanctification flourish.

Hear, O Lord, my justice : attend to my supplication. Give ear unto my prayer, which proceedeth not from deceitful lips.

Let my judgment come forth from thy countenance ; let thy eyes behold the things that are equitable.

Thou hast proved my heart, and visited it by night,

thou hast tried me by fire :

and iniquity hath not been found in me.

That my mouth may not speak the works of men : for the sake of the words of thy lips, I have kept hard ways.

our Saviour's love ?   All that we do, then, must be from God, in God, to God.   So long as we are bent on that, we need not allow ourselves to be disturbed either by the criticisms of our detractors or by scruples about our own spiritual state.

Acts : Gratitude for our common blessings, confidence in our vocation, self-abandonment to God's service.

Colloquy with God enthroned in the rules of our order.

42. Ps. XVI. (Exaudi Domine justitiam).
RESISTANCES OF OUR CORRUPT NATURE.

FIRST POINT. *The soul reminds God of his gracious dealings hitherto*.   Let us be certain, in praying against imperfections, that we pray with justice, not with deceitful lips—that is, that we do so not out of a desire for our own comfort, or for mere self-improvement, but from a real jealousy for God's honour.   Since he has begun a good work in us, we can appeal to his fidelity to bring it to its fulfilment.   He has proved our heart, and visited it by night—by the night of desolation, in which we seemed dead to sense and blind to spiritual light, save only for the fixed determination of our will. He has tried us by fire—persecutions from without, or bodily ill-health, or internal temptations : thus does he test our faithfulness.   And, through his grace thus purifying us, at least the habitual inclination to sin seemed to have been left behind. We had come to have a higher standard for ourselves than the world's standard ; mindful of his encouragement to take up the cross, we had resigned ourselves to the difficult task of self-conquest.

Perfect thou my goings in thy paths, that my footsteps be not moved.

I have cried to thee, for thou, O God, hast heard me : O incline thy ear unto me and hear my words. Shew forth thy wonderful mercies ; thou who savest them that trust in thee.

From them that resist thy right hand keep me, as the apple of an eye.

Protect me under the shadow of thy wings from the face of the wicked who have afflicted me.

My enemies have surrounded my soul : they have shut up their fat : their mouth hath spoken proudly. They have cast me forth, and now they have surrounded me ; they have set their eyes bowing down to the earth. They have taken me, as a lion prepared for the prey : and as a young lion dwelling in secret places.

Arise, O Lord, disappoint him and supplant him ;

deliver my soul from the wicked one :

thy sword from the enemies of thy hand.

O Lord, divide them from the few of the earth in their life ;

SECOND POINT. *Let us ask for present relief, if it be his will.* And yet, it seems, we are very far as yet from steady progress in the path set before us : a little less grace, and our feet would fail under us altogether, entangled in the morass. To God then, who has wrought in us so far, we must turn afresh for help ; his boundless mercy will not stop short, leaving his work half-done, if only we will trust in him. As the eyelid instinctively and immediately covers the eye when it is threatened, so we would have our souls, now consecrated to him, shrink from the merest approach of sin. As the mother-bird shelters her young, so we would have our lives hidden away from the rude touch of the world. And yet, ubiquitous and imperious, the old echoes of the world come round us ; what pain it cost us when we thought we were parting from them ! And now we find them still with us ; evil thoughts that assail us unawares, threatening to make havoc of our souls, and sullenly turn their regard downwards, away from the graces and inspirations of God.

THIRD POINT. *And we may also ask God, in his own time, to deliver us altogether from these hindrances.* May it be God's pleasure to disappoint and supplant in us the devil, who thus tries to usurp his kingdom. May he set free our souls from such tyranny ; preserve, for his own use, the sword of the Spirit which he entrusted to us, tempered so lovingly, sharpened by so much discipline, and now in danger of being dulled and blunted. The souls he chooses for the interior life are so few ; he will deliver them, surely, from the domination of nature and of the human spirit which oppresses the children of the world. There is so much misuse of God's

their belly is filled from thy hidden stores : they are full of children, and they have left to their little ones the rest of their substance. But as for me, I will appear before thy sight in justice.

I shall be satisfied when thy glory shall appear.

Hear, O Lord, my prayer : give ear to my supplication in thy truth; hear me in thy justice.

And enter not into judgment with thy servant; for in thy sight no man living shall be justified.

For the enemy hath persecuted my soul ;

he hath brought down my life to the earth ;
he hath made me to dwell in darkness
as those that have been dead of old :
and my spirit is in anguish within me : my heart within me is troubled.

own gifts, so much selfishness and calculating ambition : surely he will accept one soul that aspires to conquer herself before she appears at the judgment-seat, and centres all her hopes of happiness upon the glory which shall be revealed in Heaven.

Acts : Resignation to God's will; aspiration towards self-conquest : confidence in God and in our vocation.

Colloquy with God who has called us and will keep us for himself.

43. Ps. CXLII. (Domine exaudi ... auribus percipe). .

IMPERFECTIONS AS A HUMILIATION.

FIRST POINT. *Disheartening effect of the continued resistance of nature against our spiritual effort.* God is faithful : that is, when he makes a promise to us, however little we deserve it, he owes it to his own Nature that he should fulfil his undertaking. Thus, since he has promised that they who ask should receive, they who seek should find, etc., we can appeal, as it were, to his *justice* to make fruitful our efforts after sanctification. This is not to say that the greatest of his Saints could really claim, as a matter of retributive justice, rewards for his striving : no man, however mortified, could dare to ask God to give him his deserts. But when he gives us grace to feel our continual shortcomings as an affliction, it does mean that we may, and should, ask to be delivered from this merited affliction, which is always bringing us down into the dust, always clouding our spiritual outlook, nay, making us feel as if the very principle of perseverance were dead within us. We must avoid impatience with

I remembered the days of old : I meditated on all thy works : I meditated upon the works of thy hands.

I stretched forth my hands to thee : my soul is as earth without water unto thee.

Hear me speedily, O Lord ; my spirit hath fainted away,

turn not away thy face from me, lest I be like unto them that go down into the pit.

Cause me to hear thy mercy in the morning, for in thee have I hoped.

Make the way known to me, wherein I should walk, for I have lifted up my soul to thee.

Deliver me from my enemies, O Lord : to thee have I fled : teach me to do thy will, for thou art my God.

Thy good spirit shall lead me into the right land.

For thy name's sake, O Lord, thou wilt quicken me in thy justice.

Thou wilt bring my soul out of trouble : and in thy mercy thou wilt destroy my enemies.

ourselves, but the pain and perplexity of these humiliations is a means for us to rise higher.

SECOND POINT. *Yet this disheartening should quicken our sense of need for grace.* Let the soul look back to the time before she gave herself to God, when she was still governed by worldliness and self-will ; was it then any effort of her own, and not rather the free grace of God, that led her forward ? Now, as then, can we do more than stretch out our hands to receive a gift ? We must be like the parched ground, which, because of the drought which crumbles it, is all the more eager to drink up the moisture when it comes. Above all, let us ask for perseverance, that the weariness of our spirits may not lead to despair, that we may not come short of grace and lose our vocation. However long the night is, the morning will dawn ; however long God allows our spiritual horizon to be over-clouded with darkness, he will give the light if we wait patiently ; light and darkness, bless the Lord.

THIRD POINT. *We must also learn to let God work in his way, not in ours.* I must not be led, by impatience with myself, into attempting short cuts to holiness, I must let God reveal to me the way he has chosen for me. He knows the dispositions of the enemy's forces : I must put myself entirely under his generalship, asking him to give me the spirit of discipline, which knows how to obey without questioning. Thus, in his own time, the merciful guidance of the Holy Spirit will bring me into the promised territory. The spiritual powers that now seem numbed will be alive again, for his own Name's sake—for the glory will belong to him, not to me. The hindrances of which I now complain will be done away, or at least weakened so that they

And thou wilt cut off all them that afflict my soul,
for I am thy servant.

Give ear, O thou that rulest Israel, thou that leadest Joseph like a sheep.

Thou that sittest upon the cherubims, shine forth before Ephraim, Benjamin, and Manasses.
Stir up thy might, and come to save us.

Convert us, O God, and shew us thy face, and we shall be saved.

O Lord God of hosts, how long wilt thou be angry with the prayer of thy servant ? How long wilt thou feed us with the bread of tears, and give us for our drink tears in measure ?

Thou hast made us to be a contradiction to our neighbours, and our enemies have scoffed at us.
O God of hosts, convert us, and shew thy face, and we shall be saved.

can no longer hurt my progress. I am God's servant : is it likely that while I claim only that title and recognise only that motive, he will allow his enemies to triumph over me ?

Acts : Humble recognition of your own weakness ; faith in God's guidance ; hope for higher spiritual progress.

Colloquy with God as my guide, whose directions I must follow implicitly.

44. Ps. LXXIX. (Qui regis Israel).
Lost Fervours.

First Point. *Special grace is needed for the recovery of a soul that has grown tepid.* We should think often (as the Bible speaks often) of our souls as sheep tended, fed, and directed by the hand of a loving shepherd. Our Lord tells us that he knows his sheep by name ; he cares as much for the youngest as for the first-born, as much for the insignificant as for the great. We do not presume, then, for all our unworthiness, in asking him now for a special outpouring of grace. It is not that he has turned his face away ; we have turned our backs on him, and need to be converted, turned round, towards him. It is not wonderful if, after our neglect, he will not at once make prayer easy or pleasant to us ; he may well demand that we should spend a long time of waiting, during which all spiritual effort will be laborious and apparently unrewarded. The world we are trying to turn our backs on again will be amused at our " conversion " ; we shall get little credit from it for good resolves. But we must look towards God, in the light of whose countenance lies our only hope of salvation.

Thou hast brought a vineyard out of Egypt ; thou hast cast out the Gentiles and planted it.

Thou wast the guide of its journey in its sight ; thou plantedst the roots thereof, and it filled the land.

The shadow of it covered the hills, and the branches thereof the cedars of God ; it stretched forth its branches unto the sea, and its boughs unto the river.

Why hast thou broken down the hedge thereof, so that all they who pass by the way do pluck it ?

The boar out of the wood hath laid it waste, and a singular wild beast hath devoured it.

Turn again, O God of hosts, look down from heaven, and see, and visit this vineyard.

And perfect the same which thy right hand hath planted, and upon the son of man whom thou hast confirmed for thyself.

Things set on fire and dug down shall perish at the rebuke of thy countenance.

Let thy hand be upon the man of thy right hand, and upon the son of man whom thou hast confirmed for thyself.

SECOND POINT. *Let us remember God's past favours, and our misuse of them.* It was God, not Moses, who brought Israel out of Egypt : it was grace, not our efforts, that first brought us out of the bondage of sin, and transplanted us into a supernatural soil. By a thousand unperceived circumstances of our life God trained and tended us as the husbandman trains the vine to grow ; he fed us continually with the sap of his grace, till we became fruitful at least in good intentions. No height of perfection then seemed too high for our ambitious endeavours to aspire to ; no task he might call us to seemed out of reach of our impatient struggle for self-development. Alas ! we were not careful to keep it shielded with the wall it needed—a pure intention for his glory alone : and thus our imprudence and presumption laid it open as a prey to our spiritual enemies, who reaped the fruit meant for God ; nature, still untamed, worked havoc in us, and our ruling passion, pride or carelessness or ambition, nipped all our holy resolutions in the bud.

THIRD POINT. *Let us appeal to God that his work in us may not be left unfulfilled.* We have travelled far from God, but not out of reach of that loving eye, that all-pardoning mercy. His was the hand that began the good work in us ; he it was who strengthened and prospered us in it ; he, if we will let him, will perfect it to his own glory. There is much of our own work left that must be burned away with the fire of mortification, and dug down by more careful examination of conscience, before he can see our soul at all in the condition he wishes to find it in. In us he willed to shew forth his power; upon us, feeble and mortal creatures, he determined to bestow the supernatural aid which would

And we depart not from thee : thou shalt quicken us, and we will call upon thy name.

O Lord God of hosts, convert us, and shew thy face, and we shall be saved.

I cried to the Lord with my voice, to God with my voice, and he gave ear to me.

In the day of my trouble I sought God,
With my hands lifted up to him in the night,
And I was not deceived.
My soul refused to be comforted :

I remembered God, and was delighted, and was exercised, and my spirit swooned away.

My eyes prevented the watches ;
I was troubled, and I spoke not.

I thought upon the days of old, and I had in mind the eternal years.

help us to overcome. He never deserts any but
those who desert him ; may he confirm us in our
present intention of returning to him, and we shall
live again, and past graces will revive and bloom
once more. To him only we will attribute the
glory, as to him only we appeal for new hearts, new
light, new hopes of salvation.

Acts : Thanksgiving ; contrition ; pure intention
for God's glory.

Colloquy with God as the Gardener, who can bring
forth fruit from the barren soil of our souls.

45. Ps. LXXVI. (Voce mea ad Dominum).
THE PLACE OF TRIALS AND PERSECUTIONS.

FIRST POINT. *In time of trial, the devout soul
must throw herself all the more upon God.* We must
not for a moment think of God, even when he seems
to afford us least relief, as not hearing or not attend-
ing to our prayers. Our trials must throw us back
especially on his strength ; although in the darkness that surrounds our souls it seems as if we
could not pray, but merely go through the motions
of prayer, yet such an offering of the will cannot go
unrewarded. We must refuse all opportunities
of drowning our heaviness in worldly excitements
or dissipations. We must think of God only,
although the delight we take in the first mention of
his name gives place afterwards to anxious ques-
tionings and scruples, to a sense of impotence that
tempts us to despair. We must not curtail, but
rather forestall and prolong, if need be, the accustomed hour of prayer ; we must avoid seeking
sympathy from others for the afflictions that beset
us. We must learn to rise above our transitory
troubles by considering how God from all eternity

And I meditated in the night with my own heart, and I was exercised, and I swept my spirit.

Will God then cast off for ever ?   Or will he never be more favourable again ?

Or will he cut off his mercy for ever, from generation to generation ?

Or will God forget to show mercy ?   Or will he in his anger shut up his mercies ?

And I said, Now I have begun ;

This is the change of the right hand of the most High.

I remember the works of the Lord, for I will be mindful of thy wonders from the beginning.

And I will meditate on all thy works, and will be employed in thy inventions.

Thy way, O God, is in the holy place.   Who is the great God like our God ?   Thou art the God that dost wonders.

Thou hast made thy power known among the nations ; with thy arm thou hast redeemed thy people, the children of Jacob and of Joseph. The waters saw thee, O God, the waters saw thee, and they were afraid, and the depths were troubled.   Great was the noise of the waters, the clouds sent out a sound ; for thy arrows pass, the voice of thy thunder in a wheel.   Thy

planned our creation, and with it all the circumstances of our life. We must examine our consciences carefully, to make sure that our afflictions are not the penalty for some infidelity on our part.

SECOND POINT. *We must see, in this chastening, part of God's loving plan for us.* Is it likely that God, who has so beneficently created and preserved us, is neglecting us now, or will neglect us unless we first, by impenitence, turn away from him ? Are we to suppose that he would cut off from us, worthless as we are, the boundless supply of his mercy ? Does he forget our frailness, his faithfulness, and grow weary of our many short-comings ? Rather, this visitation is the beginning of our interior life, the first step in our spiritual education ; the hand that chastened is the same as the hand that blessed us. In all the history of God's dealings with his Saints, do we not read how he used such discipline for their good ? We cannot hope to understand all his dealings, but if we will meditate on them with resignation and suffer ourselves to be exercised by them, they will yield the fruit of justice.

THIRD POINT. *God's terrors, which frighten his enemies, leave his faithful servants unharmed.* God's ways are higher than ours, yet we can mark their beneficent operation. When he brought the children of Israel out of Egypt with a mighty hand, with what convulsions of nature this deliverance was accompanied ! The sea forgetting its natural laws, and shrinking away, as it were, from his presence ; the terrible storm of hail, with the thunder and the lightning that accompanied them, in a land where rain was almost unknown, the shaking of Mount Sinai when Moses went up to meet him there —must not all these have seemed, to the onlooker,

lightnings enlightened the world; the earth shook and trembled.

Thy way is in the sea, and thy paths in many waters, and thy footsteps shall not be known.

Thou hast conducted thy people like sheep, by the hand of Moses and Aaron.

O God, my God, to thee do I watch at break of day.

For thee my soul hath thirsted,

for thee my flesh, O how many ways!

In a desert land,
and where there is no way,
and no water,
so in the sanctuary have I come before thee,

merely the revelation of a God terrible in his anger and irresistible in his strength ? When the thunders had ceased, and the sea had rolled back, one would have supposed all this fury and commotion a meaningless display of power. And yet, through all this, we know that he was in reality guiding and protecting his people Israel, with the prudence and gentleness of a shepherd leading his flock. And shall our hearts fail at the mere whisper of his terrors ?

Acts : Abandonment of ourselves to God's care ; patience and confidence during our light afflictions.

Colloquy with God who, in his visitations, leads us like sheep.

46. Ps. LXII. (Deus, Deus meus, ad te).
DRYNESS IN PRAYER.

FIRST POINT. *Dryness in our prayers does not make them less acceptable to God.* There must be times in prayer when we feel like night-watchers at the dawn—tired, jaded, cold and hungry, only sticking to their posts out of a sheer sense of duty. So far as the will is concerned, we thirst as much as ever for union with God, yet do not experience that divine thirst of loving desire which, in some strange way, brings with it its own satisfaction : our souls are restless and distracted, and the body itself, with the imaginative faculty which is so closely allied to the body, shares this restlessness and is ill at ease. The spiritual path becomes a desert, with no sense of God's presence ; trackless, with no directing impulses of his Holy Spirit ; waterless, with no conscious devotion or apparent spiritual profit. But what matters is not the light in which our earthly journey appears to us, but the value it has

to see thy power and thy glory.

For thy mercy is better than lives ; thee my
lips shall praise.

Thus will I bless thee all my life long, and in
thy name I will lift up my hands.

Let my soul be filled as with marrow and
fatness,
and my mouth shall praise thee with joyful lips.

If I have remembered thee upon my bed, I
will meditate on thee in the morning, because
thou hast been my helper.

And I will rejoice under the covert of thy
wings ;
my soul hath stuck close to thee ;

thy right hand hath received me.

But they have sought my soul in vain ;

in the sight of God's heavenly court : are we content to draw all our strength from him, to ascribe all the glory to him ? If so, we are winning from his mercy a heavenly reward more durable and valuable than the most devout fervours we can feel in this life : our affections are not always ours to command, but we can still pray acceptably.

SECOND POINT. *We may ask for relief from such disquiet.* If it be God's will, we are content to go on worshipping in these difficult circumstances, holding up our hands in prayer when we cannot consciously lift up our hearts, if need be, all our life long. But rather, lest we be tried too hard, let it be his pleasure to deliver us, to refresh us anew in his own time with the rich banquet of his consolations ; to make the service we now pay him out of blind loyalty, natural and delightful to us. Then, in gratitude for his help, we will try to keep his presence and his glory more uninterruptedly in view, recurring lovingly to the thought of him not merely at fixed hours of prayer but whenever the regard of our minds is free to do so. Then it shall be our constant desire to be hidden away from the world in the intimacy of communion with him, to be knitted ever more closely to him with all the affection of our hearts, to derive from the consciousness of his protection all our courage in danger and all our consolation in time of trouble.

THIRD POINT. *But chiefly we must pray that our present afflictions may not tempt us to any infidelity.* At times of spiritual dryness, the devil will not be slow to suggest disloyal thoughts of revolt from the Master who seems to reward our services so little. May these machinations against our souls' safety be brought to nought by God's grace ; may they be

they shall go into the lower parts of the earth ;
they shall be delivered into the hands of the
sword ;
they shall be the portions of foxes.

But the king shall rejoice in God ;
all they shall be praised that swear by him ;

because the mouth is stopped of them that speak
wicked things.

As the hart panteth after the fountains of
water, so my soul panteth after thee, O God.

My soul hath thirsted after the strong
living God.

When shall I come and appear before the
face of God ?

buried by courageous disregard, slain by the powerful sword of the Spirit, or torn to pieces by the
remorse of an enlightened conscience. We are
resolved not to allow our souls, however distracted
from God, to find satisfaction or consolation in any
lower object : we are sworn to his service, the most
honourable service in which any creature can be
engaged ; the temptation must be gagged as soon
as it tries to make its appeal, lest by listening even
for a moment to the treacherous voice we should be
led to waver in our resolution.

Acts : Resignation to spiritual difficulties ;
renewed desire for closer union ; resolution against
the smallest infidelity.

Colloquy with God who makes the waters flow in
the wilderness.

47. Ps. XLI. (Quemadmodum desiderat).
SPIRITUAL DARKNESS.

FIRST POINT. *The soul aspires to God, who still
hides himself*. The hart flies to the streams for
safety, for coolness, to quench its thirst. In God
the soul finds her salvation, her refreshment on her
journey, the satisfaction of her spiritual desire.
But there are times when the soul, though her
thirst is undiminished, finds that her prayer is no
longer satisfied with spiritual delights ; when,
wearied and parched, she looks in vain for the cool
plunge into recollection ; when she cannot even
feel that she is in a state of grace. The thirst,
which used to meet at every breath with an answer-
ing draught of the Divine favour, now becomes a
painful exercise : how long is the time of her trial to
last, before God will admit her to a more continual
union with himself ? Her own state, her own

My tears have been my bread day and night,
whilst it is said to me daily, Where is thy God ?

These things I remembered, and poured out
my soul in me ; for I shall go over into the
place of the wonderful tabernacle, even to the
house of God ;

with the voice of joy and praise ; the noise of
one feasting.

Why art thou sad, O my soul, and why dost
thou trouble me ?   Hope in God, for I will still
give praise to him, the salvation of my countenance, and my God.

My soul is troubled within myself : therefore
will I remember thee from the land of Jordan
and Hermoniim, from the little hill.

Deep calleth on deep, at the noise of thy
flood-gates ; all thy heights and thy billows have
passed over me.

In the day-time the Lord hath commanded
his mercy, and a canticle to him in the night.

unsatisfied yearnings, fill her whole outlook with what seems a selfish absorption. And there is a devilish voice which whispers to her insistently, either that God is not, or that he has cast her off as worthless.

SECOND POINT. *In such trials, it is well to remember God's mercies in the past.* God seems to absent himself from our prayers : is there no object to which we can turn in order to feed our affections ? At least we can go back in memory to the spiritual favours of the past—transitory, indeed, like a tabernacle in the wilderness, yet full of awe and of delight, when we seemed to feel God dwelling close to us as in his temple. The outbursts of happiness, the gratitude, the banquet (though it were but of fragments) of the Divine Love . . . Can we, whom he has thus privileged, really despair of our spiritual journey, really be alarmed lest he should leave his work in us imperfect ? We dare not give up hope ; we have committed ourselves to him, and he is our God and our All. Because we have now no light, because he allows us to fall into this distress of spirit, we must remember all the more the passage of our Jordan, that is, the transferring of our affections to heavenly things, our Hermon of Transfiguration, when, though it were only for a moment, he showed us something of the brightness of his Face.

THIRD POINT. *We must pray in quietness and confidence that he would bring us out into the light again.* We must humble our heads, while the strange echoes affright us in our loneliness, and wave after wave of spiritual impotence seems to crush and annihilate us. It was, and will be, by God's mercy and God's disposition that the light visits us ; it is ours to see that in the darkness too

With me is prayer to the God of my life;
I will say to God, Thou art my support; why
hast thou forgotten me, and why go I mourning,
whilst my enemy afflicteth me? Whilst my
bones are broken, my enemies who trouble me
have reproached me;

Whilst they say to me day by day, Where is
thy God?

Why art thou cast down, O my soul? And
why dost thou disquiet me? Hope thou in
God, for I will still give praise to him, the
salvation of my countenance, and my God.

Shout with joy to God, all the earth; sing
a psalm to his name; give glory to his praise.

Say unto God, How terrible are thy works,
O Lord; in the multitude of thy strength thy
enemies shall lie to thee.

Let all the earth adore thee, and sing to thee;
let it sing a psalm to thy name.

Come and see the works of the Lord, who is
terrible in his counsels over the sons of men;

we do not fail to raise the aspiration of our wills to him. Prayer is the soul's life; while we yet live, we can pray to God who, in spite of all, never lets go his hold of us: we can remonstrate with him quietly on the exposure of our souls to spiritual assaults, as long as we remember that these are only permitted in order to crush out self and self-love and self-pride, the hard resistances of the human spirit. Days come and go, and still he tarries, but still we will not give up our hope, because we rest secure in the confidence that we have committed ourselves to him, and he is our God and our All.

Acts : Gratitude, confidence.

Colloquy with God whose arms are still beneath us, though the waves go over us and the darkness hides him.

48. Ps. LXV. (Jubilate Deo, . . . psalmum dicite).

THANKSGIVING FOR A SPIRITUAL DELIVERANCE

FIRST POINT. *God is the absolute Master of his creatures.* May the song of gratitude that now fills my heart be united with the whole chorus of praise that goes up to God continually from his creatures ! His works, even in Nature around me, are such as to fill me with awe ; it is only because of the vastness of his unchanging, unhurrying design that sinners are led to forget him and neglect him in their lives. But, where the ungodly sees nothing but blind force and purposeless wealth of detail, the devout soul recognises that everything in the world contributes finally to the praise of God. There is the same leisureliness and the same mystery in his dealings with men ; yet, to the eye of faith, his chastisements, however terrible, are still a revelation of his

who turneth the sea into dry land ; in the river they shall pass on foot ; there shall we rejoice in him.

Who by his power ruleth for ever ; his eyes behold the nations ; let not them that provoke him be exalted in themselves.

O bless our God, ye Gentiles, and make the voice of his praise to be heard ;

who hath set my soul to live, and hath not suffered my feet to be moved.

For thou, O God, hast proved us ; thou hast tried us by fire, as silver is tried.

Thou hast brought us into a net ;

thou hast laid afflictions on our back ;

thou hast set men over our heads.
We have passed through fire and water, and thou hast brought us out into a refreshment.

I will go into thy house with burnt offerings ; I will pay thee my vows, which my lips have uttered and my mouth hath spoken when I was in trouble.

purpose. The terrible waves of persecution and distress are seen to be merely the probation through which he makes a way for his redeemed to walk by. His arm is not shortened, even where men try to live without him and offend him by their neglect ; sooner or later, the pride of his enemies is shewn to be ill-grounded.

SECOND POINT. *God has shown his mastery in my own life.* As he deals with continents or with nations, so with souls ; would that all men might share the revelation he has given me of his Providence. My scruples told me that I was marked down for eternal damnation ; my fears almost persuaded me that I should never again feel solid ground under my feet. And yet in all this he did but try me and prove me, like the silver which is all the more precious for its refining in the fire till it reflects its maker's image perfectly. That I might learn to distrust myself, he let me feel myself clogged down by the claims of my corrupt nature ; he gave me mortifications, interior and exterior, which seemed as if they must break my spirit ; he allowed me to be misjudged and despised by my superiors and my fellows. My soul fought for breath, as if suffocated by the waters that ran over me, or pined for healing moisture amidst the spiritual drought that parched me. And behold ! he has brought me out into a place of refreshment, where flood and desert are at an end, where I can breathe freely again and feel his cool winds fan me.

THIRD POINT. *This deliverance should inspire me with greater fidelity.* May he enlighten my ungrateful heart, so that I may signalize this deliverance by the strict fulfilment of the vows and aspirations I made to him in the time of my trouble, promising

I will offer to thee holocausts full of marrow, with burnt offerings of rams ; I will offer to thee bullocks with goats.

Come and hear, all ye that fear God, and I will tell you what great things he hath done for my soul. I cried to him with my mouth and I extolled him with my tongue. If I have looked at iniquity in my heart, the Lord will not hear me. Therefore hath God heard me, and hath attended to the voice of my supplication.

Blessed be God, who hath not turned away my prayer, nor his mercy from me.

In my trouble I cried to the Lord, and he heard me.

O Lord, deliver my soul from wicked lips, and a deceitful tongue. What shall be given to thee, or what shall be added to thee, to a deceitful tongue ? The sharp arrows of the mighty, with coals that lay waste.

to devote my whole self to him ! There shall be no reserves, no keeping back for myself of certain cherished immortifications, no distinction between what I will and what I will not sacrifice for him. The Saints in heaven are witnesses of my deliverance, they are witnesses also of the prayers that preceded it. If I relapse again into inconsistency and half-measures, can I expect to be heard again in time of tribulation ? If God has listened to me at this time, it has been in order that he might find me more faithful to himself ; blessed be his name, who has so often seen me worthy of reprobation and banishment from himself, yet still bears with me, relieves my afflictions, and encompasses me with his mercy.

Acts : Gratitude, resignation to God's will, renewal of resolutions.

Colloquy with the divine Artificer who tempers us with the fires of tribulation.

49. Pss. CXIX., CXX., CXXI. (Ad Dominum, Levavi, Laetatus sum).

CONVERSION.

FIRST POINT. *God has rescued me from the world.* Blessed be the tribulation which turned me from the world to God ; blessed be God, who heard the prayer of one who, till prevented by his grace, could do nothing to please him. I have said farewell (and may it be for ever !) to the false standards and unreal aims of the world that lives without God, and is content to brave, without amendment, the terrible judgments which he most righteously threatens against sinners—at once the keen pangs of remorse and the desolating pains of sense. I have lived so long in an atmosphere estranged from

Woe is me, that my sojourning is prolonged ;
I have dwelt with the inhabitants of Cedar !
my soul hath been long a sojourner.

With them that hated peace I was peaceable ;
when I spoke to them they fought against me
without cause.

I have lifted up my eyes to the mountains,
from whence help shall come to me.

My help is from the Lord, who made heaven
and earth.

May he not suffer thy foot to be moved ;
neither let him slumber that keepeth thee.

Behold, he shall neither slumber nor sleep
that keepeth Israel.

The Lord is thy keeper ; the Lord is thy
protection upon thy right hand.

The sun shall not burn thee by day, nor the
moon by night.

The Lord keepeth thee from all evil ; may
the Lord keep thy soul : may the Lord keep
thy coming in and thy going out, from henceforth now and for ever.

I rejoiced at the things that were said to me,
We shall go into the house of the Lord.

God, dallying with the temptations or sins that held me prisoner, that I must needs enter the gates of my heavenly country as half a stranger, full of worldly attachments and regrets. I thought that I was living at peace in myself, when really I had only made an ignoble compromise with these spiritual enemies, which treacherously assailed my eternal salvation while I heedlessly parleyed with them. Now there is only one peace for me—the peace which is a perpetual war upon my own sins, God's enemies.

SECOND POINT. *God has brought me confidence in place of mistrust.* In making my act of faith, I have been enabled to lift up my eyes to the City of the Seven Hills, the visible centre of Christian unity. Yet my confidence reposes in nothing lower than God himself, whose throne is Heaven, and the earth his footstool. Hitherto my feet have wavered and slipped ; may he, now that he has once planted them on the rock, keep them safe by his unceasing vigilance. Too often, perhaps, I shall forget God and slumber over his errands ; he will not forget me, or be deaf when I turn to him. He will always be there to protect me, and all the more in those directions where he sees my nature to be weakest. Times of light and times of darkness will succeed one another in my soul, but, if only I am faithful, he will not allow me to presume on the one or be discouraged by the other. May he give me the grace of perseverance, that as he has granted me a happy entrance into the Church by my baptism, so he may give me a happy dismissal at the hour of my death.

THIRD POINT. *God has given me true peace in the fold of his Church.* What greater happiness could have come to me, than to have been thus given the

o

Our feet were standing in thy courts, O Jerusalem.

Jerusalem, which is built as a city which is compact together. For thither did the tribes go up, the tribes of the Lord ; the testimony of Israel, to praise the name of the Lord.

Because there seats have sat in judgment, seats upon the house of David.

Pray ye for the things that are for the peace of Jerusalem, and abundance for them that love thee ; let peace be in thy strength, and abundance in thy towers.

For the sake of my brethren and of my neighbours I spoke peace for thee : because of the house of the Lord our God I have sought good things for thee.

To thee have I lifted up my eyes, who dwellest in heaven.

Behold, as the eyes of servants are on the hands of their masters, as the eyes of the handmaid are on the hands of her mistress, so are our eyes unto the Lord our God, until he have mercy on us.

freedom of the heavenly City, the household of God ?   Planted on these rock-built foundations, I know at last what it is to stand firmly on my feet. Nor is it only the solid ground of the Apostolic faith that reassures me ; everywhere the organization of the Church speaks to me of that unity which depends on a proper relation between the members and the whole body.   Not that laws and jurisdiction are absent, but these are no tyranny, because they are loyally accepted by the free consent of the Church's children.   As a patriot of my supernatural country, I will pray earnestly for the peace of the Church, and the abundant sanctification of her children—on these two foundations rests (humanly speaking) her whole prosperity.   And I will gladly do my little part to secure that peace and to enhance those spiritual blessings, that I may be a worthy inmate of God's house and fellow-citizen of his Saints.

Acts : Gratitude, confidence, loyal submission.

Colloquy with God who watches ceaselessly over his chosen people.

50. Pss. CXXII., CXXIII., CXXIV.

(Ad te levavi, Nisi quia Dominus, Qui confidunt).

THE STRUGGLE WITH TEMPTATIONS.

FIRST POINT. *We must wait patiently for God's grace.*   I know something of my own weakness ; I have seen the failure of so many attempts at unaided effort ; now, in my hopeless imperfection, I look up to God for deliverance.   I will wait patiently, continually watching, like a king's attendant, for the least signal of God's will, trusting rather to such quiet expectation in prayer than to any violent striving on my own part, to effect my

Have mercy on us, O Lord, have mercy on us, for we are greatly filled with contempt.

For our soul is greatly filled ; we are a reproach to the rich, and contempt to the proud.

If it had not been that the Lord was with us, let Israel now say ; if it had not been that the Lord was with us, when men rose up against us, perhaps they had swallowed us alive : when their fury was enkindled against us, perhaps the waters had swallowed us up.

Our soul hath passed through a torrent ; perhaps our soul had passed through a water insupportable.

Blessed be the Lord, who hath not given us to be a prey to their teeth ; our soul hath been delivered as a sparrow out of the snare of the fowlers.

The snare is broken, and we are delivered.

Our help is in the name of the Lord, who made heaven and earth.

sanctification : God will visit me in his own time. Yet I will pray earnestly that it may be soon : for the spiritual light I have now, little as it is, is enough to make me despise myself for my own imperfections, and compare myself unfavourably with the examples of the Saints. My immortified affections, no longer (thank God) seen as friends and companions, now appear to me as hideous tyrants, mocking my feeble efforts to extricate myself from their bondage : Lord, thou seest my helplessness ; let the measure of thy assistance be in proportion to its needs.

SECOND POINT. *We must ascribe all deliverance only to his grace.* A little done towards achievement ; a little breathing-space gained in the struggle with my spiritual enemies. To what can I ascribe this, save to God's grace ? If I had been left to myself, my rebellion against the dominion of my own passions might have cost me dear : I might have lost heart altogether and been swept away, my last state worse than the first, like one swallowed up in the hosts of the enemy or carried off down a waterfall. Now the angry ford is safely bridged, and I am on firm land again : I no longer feel myself snared and limed like a captive bird by the clogging attachment of some immortified passion that I had almost given up hope of escaping. It is not that I have found my way out between the bars ; the prison-cage itself has been shattered by a greater Power : the temptation is no longer felt as a temptation—this, surely, is God's doing. God, who made heaven and earth and conserves all things in being, made me to serve him and gives me from moment to moment grace to accomplish my mission.

They that trust in the Lord shall be as Mount Sion; he shall not be moved for ever that dwelleth in Jerusalem. Mountains are round about it ; so the Lord is round about his people from henceforth now and for ever.

For the Lord will not leave the rod of sinners upon the lot of the just, that the just may not stretch forth their hands to iniquity.

Do good, O Lord, to those that are good, and to the upright of heart.

But such as turn aside into bonds, the Lord shall lead out with the workers of iniquity. Peace upon Israel.

When the Lord brought back the captivity of Sion, we became like men comforted. Then was our mouth filled with gladness, and our tongue with joy. Then shall they say among

THIRD POINT. *We must have confidence in this protection.* The Christian is as " a city set on a hill " ; he is open to criticism from every side, and nothing that he does can be without its spiritual significance. Yet he is also a city set among the hills, nestling safely in the embrace of an eternal Providence. We are so open to the influence of human respect, so weak in our efforts to rise above the low standards we see around us, that we may well be alarmed as to our chances of ever living for God ; yet we must not (on pain of infidelity) doubt his power to elevate us to any height of sanctity, though we are in ourselves so closely akin to the greatest of sinners. What he requires of us is a true and honest intention of doing everything to his glory ; for the rest, we must trust to him to make what he wills of us, not enquiring anxiously about our own spiritual state. And we must pray above all for perseverance, lest we should be led at any time to look back with affectionate regret towards the sins we have escaped from, so running the risk of losing our eternal peace.

Acts : Dependence, gratitude, confidence.

Colloquy with God, who does all things in us according to his will.

51. Pss. CXXV., CXXVI., CXXVII. (In convertendo, Nisi Dominus, Beati omnes).

SPIRITUAL FRUIT.

FIRST POINT. *The spirit of captivity.* For all true interior progress we need the spirit of captivity, which embraces, by an act of the will, a rule for our daily actions and a deliberate direction of our affections and thoughts, against the inclinations of nature, which chafes at being thus cramped

the heathen, The Lord hath done great things for them.

The Lord hath done great things for us; we are become joyful.

Turn again our captivity, O Lord, as a stream in the south.

They that sow in tears shall reap in joy. Going, they went and wept, casting their seeds; but coming, they shall come with joyfulness, carrying their sheaves.

Unless the Lord build the house, they labour in vain that build it.

Unless the Lord keep the city, he watcheth in vain that keepeth it.

It is vain for you to rise before light; rise after you have sitten, you that eat the bread of sorrow.

When he shall give sleep to his beloved,

behold, the inheritance of the Lord are children, the reward, the fruit of the womb.

and confined. Only after this, only when God sees fit, these contradictions of our natural bent will become, instead of irksome, grateful and simple to us. What happiness that will be for us, what a blow to our spiritual enemies ! We must remember that this ready acquiescence in our own spiritual good is not ours by right or by merit, but a free gift of God. When the drudgery of perseverance in prayers, mortifications etc. that are painful to us turns into the happiness of willing service, it is like a stream of water suddenly flowing in the wilderness —an act of his power. Yet, commonly at least, it is not presumptuous for us to think that the happiness will come as the reward of the drudgery, and will be in proportion to the labour and the difficulty which have exercised and disciplined us ; the tears of our mortification do really water and make fruitful the seeds God's grace has sown in us.

SECOND POINT. *The need of discretion.* The edifice of perfection cannot be planned by human device ; its architecture is God's. Nay, even the process of watchful custody of the senses, whereby we guard against our imperfections, is fruitless except in so far as God furthers our endeavours. Hence we must not be in a hurry over our spiritual progress ; must not wear ourselves out with impatient and sometimes presumptuous efforts at self-improvement. Rather, we must try to reach by interior prayer that resignation of our own wills which allows God to make known to us, as in a vision of the night, his more perfect will for us. As God grants or withholds the gift of issue to marriage, so he distributes in his own time and in his own measure the graces that are acquired in prayer. Yet those graces will be truly ours ; and, as the

As arrows in the hand of the mighty, so the children of them that have been shaken; blessed is the man that hath filled his desire with them; he shall not be confounded when he shall speak to his enemies in the gate.

Blessed are all they that fear the Lord, that walk in his ways.

For thou shalt eat the labours of thy hands; blessed art thou, and it shall be well with thee.

Thy wife as a fruitful vine on the sides of thy house; thy children as olive plants, round about thy table.

Behold, thus shall the man be blessed that feareth the Lord : may the Lord bless thee out of Sion, and mayst thou see the good things of Jerusalem all the days of thy life, and mayst thou see thy children's children, peace upon Israel.

father of many children is safe against assault or judicial oppression, so he who has made progress in prayer will find comfort in the day when he stands at the Judgment-seat.

THIRD POINT. *Spiritual advancement makes us blessed even in this life.* It might seem as if living in a holy dread of God's judgments, walking in a narrow way between clearly defined landmarks, would mean an anxious and scrupulous life in this world. It is not so. The husbandman who lives on his own produce will have to work hard, but he will be independent of his neighbours for his living : so our hard spiritual discipline will make us, in our degree, independent of worldly comforts and consolations—the surest road to happiness. The soul will be like a well-ordered household or a well-trained garden—all its elements properly balanced and harmonized, and therefore at peace. The only true happiness is peace of mind. And what if we seem to be isolated, cut off from the current of worldly events ? We know that our prayers go up to God in his holy temple, calling down blessings on the faithful, winning new children for the Church, increasing the harmony and well-being of the Christian family.

Acts : Resolution to persevere through discouragement : resignation : gratitude to God for calling us to an interior life.

Colloquy with Christ as the Gardener of our souls.

Often have they fought against me from my youth, let Israel now say : often have they fought against me from my youth, but they could not prevail over me.

The wicked have wrought upon my back, they have lengthened their iniquity.

The Lord who is just will cut the necks of sinners : let them all be confounded and turned back that hate Sion.

Let them be as grass upon the tops of houses, which withereth before it be plucked up, wherewith the mower filleth not his hand, nor he that gathereth sheaves his bosom :

and they that passed by have not said, The blessing of the Lord be upon you ; We have blessed you in the name of the Lord.

Out of the depths I have cried to thee, O Lord ; Lord, hear my voice ; let thy ears be attentive to the voice of my supplication.

If thou, O Lord, wilt mark iniquities, Lord, who shall stand it ?

For with thee there is merciful forgiveness, and by reason of thy law I have waited for thee, O Lord.

52. Pss. CXXVIII., CXXIX., CXXX.(Saepe expugnaverunt, De profundis, Domine non est)

SELF-ABANDONMENT.

FIRST POINT. *Outward affections mortified.* Often, from my youth upward, the temptations that rose from inordinate affection to sense, to the world, to human respect have battered at the gates of my soul ; often they have effected a partial entry, but through God's grace they have never occupied the citadel. Yet my long subjection to those tyrannous onslaughts left my soul a prey to worldly and sensual attachments. Now, as it seems, God has struck at the very nerve-centre of these my spiritual enemies, and deadened their power to affect me ; may he grant of his mercy that this rout may be a final defeat. It is my earnest desire that the very thought, the very lingering memory of what once troubled me so deeply may now be as short-lived as the self-sown grass that withers in the sun, passing away at once from my imagination before I find any delight in it, far less give it any consent. May I pass by my temptations as a man passes by some hated enemy, without a sign of recognition or a word of greeting.

SECOND POINT. *Self unveiled.* Now, as I hope, I have descended in my prayer to the very roots of my being ; and from that abyss of humiliation cry out to the God who now seems infinitely distant. In my own self, my own rebellious human spirit, I now find nothing but blackness and rottenness where before I was conscious of nothing amiss ; if we could see sin with God's eyes, which of us would dare to hope for salvation ? And yet God gives us hope in our moments of deepest abjection ;

My soul hath relied on his word, my soul hath hoped in the Lord; from the morning watch even until night, let Israel hope in the Lord.

Because with the Lord there is mercy, and with him plentiful redemption, and he shall redeem Israel from all his iniquities.

Lord, my heart is not exalted, nor are my eyes lofty.

Neither have I walked in great matters, nor in wonderful things above me.

If I was not humbly minded, but exalted my soul :—

As a child that is weaned is towards his mother, so reward in my soul.

Let Israel hope in the Lord, from henceforth now and for ever.

his law for us is still that we should wait patiently upon his grace, and so I will ; as I trusted him in the first days of my interior progress, the days of wearisome vigilance, so I will trust him now, whatever night of dereliction and self-despair he may bring down upon my soul. His mercy and the merits of my Saviour's precious Blood do not stop short at the conversion of abandoned sinners ; there is grace to spare for perfecting devout souls, and removing the last traces of self-will, self-praise, self-pity and self-love.

THIRD POINT. *Self abandoned.* Lie still, then, my soul, under the hand of God. If ever I have congratulated myself on spiritual progress, if ever I have compared myself favourably with my neighbours, I was wrong. If ever I desired the interior life from the hope of receiving some special illumination, or of being favoured by great supernatural gifts, I was wrong. I am nothing, I came from nothing ; I dare not so much as lift up my eyes to heaven. Only, as the child that is now weaned from the breast still clings for all comfort and all love to the mother who once fed him, so my soul, weaned away by God's grace from inordinate affection to his creatures and to all that is less than him, still turns towards the Author of those gifts as her only centre and her only ground of confidence. Lord, let me continue always in this act of self-distrust and of confidence in thee, till through thy mercy I see thee face to face in Heaven, and lose myself and find myself in thee.

Acts : Humiliation and abandonment of self into the hands of God.

Colloquy with God who is all things to our nothingness.

www.ingramcontent.com/pod-product-compliance
Lightning Source LLC
Chambersburg PA
CBHW031511040426
42445CB00009B/170